Wounds

to

Wisdom

I'm Still Standing

By

Tamiko Lowry

The Writers' Magic Books
THE UNITED STATES OF AMERICA
ATLANTA, GEORGIA

Wounds to Wisdom...
I'm Still Standing

Surviving Domestic Abuse & Discovering Essential Wellness
Principles to Help You Live a Winning Lifestyle
with Still Standing Foundation Founder & Certified Life Coach Tamiko Lowry

Wounds

to

Wisdom

I'm Still Standing

Written by

TAMIKO LOWRY

Founder of Still Standing Foundation

Wounds to Wisdom...
I'm Still Standing

The Writers' Magic Books
Family & Relationships/Domestic Partner Abuse/Personal Memoir

Published By Tamiko Lowry
Permissions Granted by:
Tamiko Lowry
Cover design by The Writers' Magic Design Team
Front & Back Cover Photo by Cornell McBride Photography
Photos by Michael Sharp Photography
Other Photo Credits:
Nspired Events Photography
Photo Journeys Photography
Photo Journeys Photography by Krystal Harris
Interior Design, Digital Formatting & Typesetting by The Writers' Magic (Atlanta, GA)

LIBRARY OF CONGRESS CATALOGING –IN-PUBLICATION DATA
Tamiko Lowry

Wounds to Wisdom: I'm Still Standing
p. cm.
ISBN: 978-0-9894720-4-3

For more information, author contact or creative rights release contact:
The Writers' Magic
c/o Tamiko Lowry, The Writers' Magic
PO Box 568022
Sandy Springs, GA 31156
admin@thewritersmagic.com

First Edition Publication (Black & White Print)

Printed in the USA
9 8 7 6 5 4 3 2 1

Wounds to Wisdom...I'm Still Standing

By Tamiko Lowry

EMPOWERING YOU TO BE EMPOWERED

You are **loved**,
You are **wonderfully made**,
You are **beautiful**,
You have **purpose**,
You are a **Masterpiece**,
God has a great plan for you!

THIS BOOK HAS BEEN GIFTED TO

_____

FROM

_____

ON

_____

FOR THE BLESSINGS OF

True survivorship in all areas of your life.

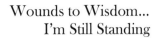

A Tamiko Lowry Brand Original

Books/eBooks/Audio Books/Speaker Training Resources and More

<u>Dedications</u>

This book is dedicated to all of the survivors in the world.

There is purpose behind the pain. God will turn your wounds into wisdom and one day you will say

"Wow; I'm Still Standing!"

No matter what it is you go through in life, remember that all things work together for the good for those who love God and who are called according to his purpose.

Romans 8:27-29

Acknowledgements

I want to personally thank the following people and organizations for their contributions to my inspiration, knowledge and help in writing this book.

My Heavenly Father: Thank you for the life lessons that gave me strength and perseverance. Thank you for allowing me to turn my wounds into wisdom and my pain into purpose. *Because of you,* I am Still Standing. You alone are my rock and my salvation. You are my fortress. I shall not be moved. *Psalm 62:2.*

Ingrid Allen: Thank you for being my writing coach and believing in my vision from the first day we spoke. Thank you for praying with & for me, and for also being my motivator—constantly reminding me of my calling.

Bishop Jonathan Alvarado: Thank you for preaching a life changing sermon on August 9th 2009. That sermon revealed my life's purpose. On that day, I became free. I was no longer a victim but a *survivor.*

Dr. Toni Alvarado: Thank you for being a mentor, coach and friend. I admire your tenacity, and wisdom. You are a true example of a woman of Proverbs 31.

Mom: Thank you for giving me the gift of life. Thank you for always supporting and encouraging my dreams. Your cards and inspirational words always put a smile on my face. You always let me know that I could do all things through Christ.

Dad: Thank you for cheering me on every day. Your text messages and phone calls gave me strength to keep pushing.

My Babies (Destiny and Michael): My shining stars! Thank you for being understanding and never judging me. Thank you for always supporting my dreams and being a part of the vision. You are truly the reason why I work so hard.

Kenny Pugh: Thank you for being my *"number one fan"* ...as you would say. You inspire me to be greater. Thank you for your words of encouragement and for sharing The Rising Star Award with me. I appreciate you!

To my business/social network, extended friends and family: Thank you for your continued support.

And last but most *certainly not* least, I would like to give a 'Special Thanks' to the volunteers, supporters and staff members of the Still Standing Foundation for your dedication to true survivorship for all...together we are *"Still Standing"*.

-Tamiko Lowry

[Wounds to Wisdom...I'm Still Standing 2014]

Knowingly, I Stand...

I stand because I know who I am.
I stand because I was wonderfully made with a purpose.
I stand because through that purpose I will fulfill my destiny.

For author events/appearances and other
information about Tamiko Lowry

Log onto
www.tamikolowry.com

Contents...

PREFACE

FORWORD *by Dr. Toni G. Alvarado*

INTERMISSION for the 'Inner'mission

Photo Highlights-Events

About the Author –Tamiko Lowry

Appendix: Wounds to Wisdom...I'm Still Standing

Stand strong by realizing your vision, understanding your calling, overcoming your obstacles and pursuing your passions.

-Tamiko Lowry

Author, CEO/Founder of SSF, Certified Life Coach

Wounds to Wisdom...
I'm Still Standing

WOUND

•   •   •   •   •

MERRIAM-WEBSTER DEFINES A WOUND AS

An injury in which the surface of something is torn,
pierced, cut, or otherwise broken.
Hurt.

He heals the brokenhearted and binds up their wounds.

Psalm 147:3

"The human race tends to remember the abuses to which it

has been subjected rather than the endearments.

What's left of kisses? Wounds, however, leave scars."

— Bertolt Brecht

 by
Dr. Toni G. Alvarado

Richard J. Leider and David A. Shapiro in their book, *Repacking Your Bags: Lighten Your Load for The Rest of Your Life*, suggest that fear is the most common emotion that people are walking around with every day. It is such a common emotion that many people have learned to function with it and never challenge the basis of their fears. Fear is such a strong emotion that people would rather stay in situations that are destructive and non-productive rather than pursue the blessings that lie beyond the borders of their fears.

Fear blinds us to life's possibilities. Fear limits us and keeps us living within the status quo. When examined closely we often discover that the things and events we fear will simply never happen. Yet, because of the fear that we allow to shape our realities we often forfeit our dreams and passions and settle for a nominal existence and non-resistant path. The Bible gives us a prescription for fear and challenges us to overcome fearful thoughts, behaviors and attitudes. The fear that the Bible speaks of is a healthy fear and reverence for God and life. *"The spirit that God gave us does not make us timid, but gives us power, love and a sound mind"* 2 Timothy 1:7. The type of fear that paralyzes us and keeps us from being our best self is simply not the way God intends for us to live our lives. Our lives were never designed to fear people particularly those whom we have close relationships with such as spouses, friends and family members.

Every now and then you will meet someone who has the courage to go beyond the borders of their fear. Yet, fewer people leave the boundaries of their fear and go back to bring others with them. As the CEO of the Still Standing Foundation, Tamiko Lowry speaks from her own experiences with domestic violence and abuse teaching women of all ages and walks of life how to avoid and release themselves from such bondage. I am excited to write the foreword for this ground-breaking book written by Tamiko Lowry on behalf of women who have survived some of life's most difficult challenges.

Many of us know someone who has been negatively impacted by a domestic violence situation. This is one of the ills of our society that knows no boundaries. It spans women of all cultures, races, occupations, income levels, and ages. In fact, statistics reveal some heartbreaking realities concerning domestic violence in America.

Consider the facts listed below:

- 1 in 4 women will experience domestic violence in their lifetime.

- 1 out of 3 of all female homicide victims are killed by a current of former intimate partner.

- More than 3 million children witness domestic violence every year.

- Domestic violence is the 3rd leading cause of homelessness in the United States.

- Most cases of domestic violence are never reported.

- Many women tend to stay in abusive relationships because of conflicting emotions or reliance on the abuser.

With statistics like these, Tamiko Lowry's book *Wounds to Wisdom, I'm Still Standing* is a timely book for everyone in our community to read.

Tamiko is very transparent in this book about her own childhood experiences of various forms of abuse. She has been willing to uncover her own wounds and share the nuggets of wisdom she has gleaned from these experiences that followed her into her adult married life.

You will find practical tools toward wholeness laced throughout this book as Tamiko prepares a journey for her readers that will lead them down a path that heals their wounds and opens up into a world of wisdom.

Domestic violence and sexual assault are generational curses that need to be broken over the lives of so many women. In this book Tamiko gives insights into breaking the generational curses of abuse and rape. So passionate is Tamiko about bringing people together in her community to aid in the healing process of those who have been abused, she has created and administrates and entire organization dedicated to helping women overcome their fears and move forward with their lives through the Still Standing Foundation. She is taking a huge risk in hopes that at least one woman would gain courage and envision a better life for herself.

You are loved.
You are wonderfully made.
You are beautiful.
You have purpose.
You are a masterpiece.
God has a great plan for you.

Preface

Though Wounded, I Was Not Destroyed...
I'm Still Standing

T hink of a young child playing on a playground... as she runs, jumps and climbs she is so filled by the joy of interacting with the other children that the excitement of the moment brings laughter to her spirit and a smile upon her face—so of course she doesn't consider that she will get hurt.

Then suddenly, another child comes over and pushes her down (mistakenly or intentional). She falls to the ground badly scraping her knee which causes her so much pain that she begins to cry. Naturally, her mother runs to her aid to console her; cleaning the wound, carefully bandaging it. Then over time, nurturing the wound until it one day heals.

However, as she grew older the scar remained as a reminder of that day on the playground. Though she tried everything that she could to try to make it fade nothing has ever made it disappear. So, she just frustratingly conceals it.

Many of us are like the little girl in the story, throughout the course of our lives we are often faced with many situations and circumstances that may cause us to become wounded—*physically, emotionally, mentally, financially and even spiritually.* These bumps and bruises we tend to carry with us along our journey; which seem to never go away—I can honestly say that I have experienced my share.

Being born to teenage parents in the mid-seventies [who lacked financial resources and education], positioned me to spend my early years growing up in a poverty-stricken neighborhood housing project on the west side of Buffalo, NY.

As a child, I witnessed a lot and suffered through many hardships due to the plaguing effects of drugs and alcoholism within my family. Seeing as though my childhood left the stage somewhat "unset" for my adult life's feature production, I set my sights on finding all of those things that I felt deprived of... *love, happiness and stability*—which sometimes lead me in all the wrong places.

Needless to say, though I struggled with the pressures of life I was forced to come face-to-face with challenges; which landed me the winning star role in this production that I call my life—'*Wounds to Wisdom*'.

Wisdom makes me stronger...
I'm Still Standing

identify:// Generally, when we speak about *wounds* we tend to gravitate toward thinking about only the physical wounds. However, we must consider that we are made up of more than just physical mass. Therefore, wounding may occur as matters of the heart (*emotional*), matters of the mind (*mental*), matters of the soul (*spiritual*) or matters of our livelihood (*financial*)—all of which can affect our overall wellness. By properly identifying with all areas of your life you will begin to discover the essential tools needed along your journey toward the peacefulness of true survivorship.

source:// It's important that we take full responsibility for examining the anatomy of our wounds, so that we will grasp ahold of and embrace the true power of our healing and wellness. Gaining an understanding of the source of our wounds also helps us to become more aware of *"clear-and-present danger"*. In other words, by recognizing repetitive source patterns we become more mindful of our choices in the present.

Though our wounds may derive from many sources [intentional or unintentional] and in some cases have a lingering painful effect, they serve as learning scars that teach us throughout our journey to wisdom.

Consider the Source:

... **Wounds of adolescence.**

... **Wounds from generational curses.**

... **Wounds in which we inflict upon ourselves.**

... **Wounds that we accept from our family members or from those that we allow to have a direct connection to us.**

I will stand strong in the midst of my challenges and struggles because I believe in my future.
I'm Still Standing

When I realized that I was a *'wounded woman walking'*, I began to search for the source of my wounds. Carefully examining each one in its own place-in-time throughout my journey. Whether self-inflicted or due to the unfortunate acts of others, the result of injury proved to be unfavorable; leaving me *bound* in confusion, anger and sometimes placed in distressed positions.

But, the good news is... I didn't remain there. I've moved forward; with a newness of my thoughts, actions and reactions. Believing in the power of healing, deliverance and restoration. Standing purposefully in the mission of survival all while directing my thoughts toward the true meaning of love, life and the *pursuit of happiness.*

inspiration:// As I look back over my life I still think of all the times I wondered…*how?* and *Why Me?* But, as I began to grow *'with'* God and *'in'* God the vision became apparent. I'm still standing! Standing to share this testament of my personal journey to offer love, hope and faith to those that are experiencing or have experienced the unfortunate acts of domestic violence.

closure:// When you are dealing with pain and are looking for closure, you have to dig deep. You will have to revisit a place and time that you are afraid to go to. But, if you really want to heal, you have to face it head on. Go back to your childhood and reminisce on the looks the feels, the smells and the sounds. Use your senses to feel the pain, the happiness, the joy, the hurt, the love. As you allow yourself to feel, you will begin to heal.

survivorship:// As I sat down each day to write I thought of each survivor out there that too, like me—were uncertain that they would live through it all. I also cried for those that lost their lives and prayed without ceasing for the families that were left to pick up all the pieces. It is through all the challenges and the hurdles that I learned the value of inspiration, which ultimately helped me along the way. So it's here that I stand, grounded within my mission for change and survivorship for all.

Wounds to Wisdom...

I'm Still Standing

The thing you fear most has no power.
Your fear of it is what has the power.
Facing the truth really will set you free.

Chapter One
MOST BEAUTIFUL CHILD

The mighty spirit of angel with a calling of destiny...

On April 19, 1975 the most beautiful little girl was born.
Her name is of Japanese origin which means most beautiful child,
or child of many beauties. At birth her head was in the shape of a
heart. It has been said that those born with a heart shaped face or
head are natural born nurturers. They are full of aspiration and
have a generous heart. She was purposed to bring peace and love
to the world. But, before she walked into her purpose she had to
endure many wounds; which would eventually turn into wisdom.
The wisdom in which she brings to the world as a means to
empower those who come in her path.

~ ~ ~

The Triumph of a Wounded Woman'—Wounds to Wisdom

Something about the name Tamiko

As I begin this new journey on *April 19, 2014*, I
pay homage to the day that I was born and named
Tamiko... April 19, 1975. //Tamiko-of Japanese origin,
which means beautiful child or child of many
beauties.//I greet you all in love. For those that know
the true meaning and purpose of their calling I walk
with you; and together we will all stand in prayer with
those that are searching for a purpose-filled destination.
Though I am who I am today—I've grown from my

roots, and I *stand* to say that I am not who I was yesterday. Life has a way of teaching us through our triumphs, trials and tragedies. Ultimately, helping us to get to know ourselves from the inside out [Wisdom].

I wanted to start this book with my *beginnings* because of the significance of 'the beginning'. In the beginning, God created [...] based on purpose; *let's begin with the creation.* It is here, that we are crafted and destined into our own purposeful mission. It's also in our beginnings that we grow into our opinions about life and learn the basic fundamentals of survivorship.

The creation of Tamiko began with love, purpose and hope—Just as with each one of you. Our bloodline, our birth, our names, our childhood experiences, are all important factors that hold key insight into who we are...*mind, body and spirit.*

Therefore, by examining the beginning we will be able grasp a clear understanding of our present actions while moving forward toward our future blessings. The beginning also helps us to gain insight into the *how's* and the *why me's*, so that we begin to understand our purpose.

Our beginning mark our roots for the route of our journey. It can also determine how we structure and conduct our lives as adults. Whether we will settle on becoming a product of our environment or choose to empower the environment.

I was created in love, purpose and hope.
I'm Still Standing

Both of my parents were teenagers when I was
born—my mother fifteen and my father eighteen—so
of course they were still learning *how* to grow into
adulthood [*Babies having babies*]. They were young,
inexperienced, dependent, lacking education and skill
which made it difficult to find jobs to provide for me.
So, my mom and I lived with my grandmother [along
with my mom's six other siblings and their children] in
a small unit of a four-story brick building, located on
the Westside of Buffalo, NY—the Jefferson Projects.

During the early years of my life I spent a lot of
time in my grandmother's care, whom I referred to as
'*Ma*'. But, respectfully, I called my mother by her first
name until I was fourteen; primarily because we were
both being raised by my grandmother. So to me, she
became more like a sister.

Although my dad lived in the same housing
project, I don't recall seeing much of him to really get
to know him. However, I do remember things like his
service in the military. But, as a pre-teen I learned that
he fathered two other children in the same year that I
was born. So, I guess you could say *"papa was a rolling
stone..."*

As a young girl, I remember the hardships, the
struggles and not to mention the overcrowding in my

grandmother's small, yet humble apartment. Arguments over *bathroom time, telephone time...* and of course *television time* was all a part of a typical day. There was never really a dull moment. Seeing as though there were so many of us in the semi-cluttered unit, there was always something going on. Which made it hard for me to really get to know my mother as *my mother*. But, as I got older, [and a little wiser] I began to view it all in a new light.

There is no place like 'home'...

When mom decided to leave Buffalo [taking me in tow] to relocate to Washington, DC with her boyfriend, I'm sure my grandmother had her reservations. All I can say is that I don't remember *too much* about living in DC. But, I do remember attending kindergarten and living in a neighborhood with lots of kids. The community seemed to be close-knit and family oriented.

The other thing that I recall was my mom's boyfriend being *very* abusive to her. Watching this man yell at my mom while beating her over and over again was a nightmare. It became hard to watch my mother try to fight back screaming for her life. In my heart, I hated him. I literally thought he was going to kill us. What was even worse was he would end each fight saying *'I love you'*.

There were many times that I would run to our neighbor's house for help. This went on for about a year before my mom decided that *enough-was-enough*. We got on the Greyhound bus back to Buffalo to our family. *I felt safe again.*

As a little girl, I always imagined myself being one of the characters that I admired in movies and on TV. This was my way of escaping reality.

While living in DC watching my mom go through abuse, I wished that I could help her. I would put on my Wonder Woman pajamas while twirling around hoping that I would turn into a super hero to save my mom from her abusive boyfriend. There were also times when I would pretend to be Dorothy from the Wizard of Oz. I would put on my favorite shoes and click my heels together chanting to myself, *"There is no place like home…There's no place like home."* When my mom told me that we were moving back to Buffalo, I thought that it was because of me clicking my heels together and chanting, *"There is no place like home."*

"I have the power to change my life."
I'm Still Standing

Identifying a "place called home."

–Home is where we feel most grounded and safe. It gives us a sense of stability and helps us to feel free. It is the sanctuary that houses our 'temple'. The place of supplication where we break bread with our families. Our haven of love, morals, instruction and support.

For a child, having a *safe* place to call home is essential to help support the idea of stability. It teaches children that *'home'* should be a nurturing place of peace and rest, which helps them to grow. However, if 'home' is a place of violence a child may begin to feel fearful, resentful, grudging, and intimidated. Which ultimately perpetuates a desire to become hurt, withdrawn, and rebellious; trying to find a way of escape.

Did you Know?

Domestic Violence occurs in every five out of ten households in the United States of America; three of which go unreported.

The Still Standing Foundation research study, Tamiko Lowry

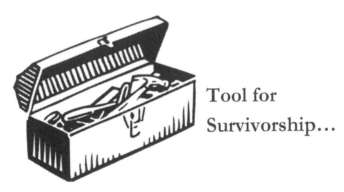 Tool for
Survivorship...

Journaling

Journaling helps us to release our thoughts and emotions. It can be a therapeutic tool that helps us along our journey. It offers clear structure in our goal setting and serves as an inspirational resource as we revisit to review our progression.

As I begin to journal my thoughts I will see my progress.
From this day forward I proclaim that my life will never be the same.
I'm Still Standing

_____

_____

_____

_____

_____

_____

_____

_____

_____

_____

_____

_____

_____

_____

_____

_____

_____.

_____

_____

_____

_____

_____

_____

_____

_____

_____

_____

_____

_____

_____

_____

_____

_____

_____

_____

_____

*Date:*_____

Today marks the first day of a lifetime of Survivorship.

Chapter Two

THE CURSE

"The Gift of The Curse"—Wisdom

"The curse became a gift ...*through the wounds of our lineage we obtained wisdom to grow into the course of our lives.*"

Though many of us may know of various events within our past ancestral history that can symbolize a generational curse, there are others that may not. Therefore, I felt it was important to write this chapter.

When we speak about *curses,* we may tend to think about some sort of 'witch-crafty' hex or a 'bad luck' black cloud—*if there is such a thing.* Generational curses are generally classified as ailments that are passed down to us from our generational past. History, which repeats itself over time through ancestry.

Getting to know the Source. Three known generations of women caught in the web of domestic abuse inflict a wound upon a girl-child; that at birth, had no knowledge of abuse or what it means to be abused. This young women, entering into her coming of age, remembers the earful pain of the cries from her mother. She also revisits the helplessness of inferiority and the shattering of a loving ideal. As she searches for the *how's* and *why's,* she finds that she has been subliminally taking along the emotion from the abuse; carrying it mind, body and spirit throughout her [now] adult life.

The Source marks the 'cause' that can influence our 'effect'.

Seeing as though my mother had me at such a young age I really don't believe that she really knew how to play the role of a mother; she was still just a child herself. There were times when she was abusive to me, both verbally and physically. For years, I thought... maybe she did those things because she didn't like me? She would yell at me, beat me and would tell me how she wishes she would have aborted me.

Those words stung and stayed with me for years to come. I don't think she understood the depth to which she hurt me. She was young and only acting out what she saw in her own life.

Her father (my grandfather) was very abusive. I remember watching him beat his wife if she literally blinked the wrong way. He would call her –'stupid bitches'—and all types of degrading names.

He also had two sons—that he would also beat. He beat them like they were 'wild animals'. I even recall a few times when he beat his wife with a waist belt.

Although he treated me like a princess and never hit or yelled at me, I was still afraid of him.

Abuse was a generational curse in my family. My great grandmother was abused. My grandmother was abused. My mother was abused. My grandfather was abusive (pretty much all of my mother's side of the family). To us, it was normal way of life.

Both sides of my family would always cuss one another out... *without thinking twice about it*. Even when I would visit my dad's side of the family, they too would cuss at one another like it was normal.

My father became 'a pimp' and 'a hustler', so it wasn't a big thing for him to disrespect women—and I was no exception to the rule. There were times that I would see him parade around the city wearing fur coats and beautiful women on his arms.

Though I became very quiet, shy and somewhat distant as a child, I paid very close attention to my surroundings (I seen a lot and learned a lot). Even at a very young age I knew what a pimp and a prostitute was. Primarily, because most of the men that I looked up to abused their girlfriends, wives and families; treating them like trash.

Today, I break all generational curses from my life,
the lives of my children and my future bloodline.
I'm Still Standing...

Survival Talk-

TOPIC *of* DISCUSSION:

- *What do the words 'generational curse' mean to you?*
- *Do you know your family history?*
- *Do your feel as though your life has been influenced by a generational curse?*
- *Breaking every curse that comes upon our lives.*

Chapter Three

DANCE LIKE
NO ONE IS WATCHING

"Dance into your rhythm of life!"- Tamiko Lowry

I loved being with my grandmother aka 'Momma' [or Ma, as I referred to her]. She always seemed so happy. Her smile would light up a room and her hugs would send love shock vibes all throughout my small-framed body. For the most part, the words that came from her lips were encouragingly sweet. However, she knew just how to get her point across when it came to reprimand. I still say her *words of wisdom* planted seeds of instruction that have blossomed in my mind over time, helping me to become the woman that I am today.

My fondest memories were being at her house and the entire family would come over to 'party'. My grandmother was known for throwing *the best* house parties in the neighborhood. She was so full of energy.

I can remember, (just as if it were yesterday) a Marvin Gaye song would be playing in the background while the adults played card games, talking *'trash-talk'* to one another. Then, to make it more interesting they would have dance contests; which always featured the infamous "Soul Train Line" from the American musical variety show Soul Train. Of course I would never participate because I was so shy. *But*...enjoyed watching and listening to the music.

The music...*Oh yes,*—the music. The music of the 70's and 80's gave us all a sense of emotion and freedom. It voiced the pleasures love and moaned the heartache of pain. Furthermore, it had its way of making you feel the beat of hope, which compelled you to dance.

Dancing is an ageless universal language of expression that holds the rhythm of life in every step. There was just something about dancing. I'll never forget the first time I danced. It was at my 7th birthday party that I danced to Michael Jackson's hit song Billie Jean. I jumped out of my seat and [figuratively speaking] *'tore the dance floor up'*. I recall being in *love* with Michael Jackson. Funny, but I thought for sure he would be my husband one day—me, and a lot of other seven year old girls all over the world; *I'm sure.*

I truly thank [the late & great] Michael Jackson for bringing me out of my shell of shyness by inspiring my love for dancing. It helped me to express myself.

Shortly after the party, my mom realized my love and passion for dance, so she enrolled me in a dance school; where I took Tap Dance, Jazz and Ballet for the next several years. Whenever we would have family gatherings my mom would always bring my tap shoes and make me do a tap dance routine for the family. Dancing was very therapeutic for me. It still is today. Whenever I feel sad, depressed, or stressed, I dance like no one is watching.

"I will find my rhythm while dancing within my freedom."

I'm Still Standing

Throughout life we all have passions that lie deep within that are suppressed by our fears. Fear can hold us back from living our purpose causing us to live life in complacency. Therefore, it is important to take some time out for self-inventory.

Reflect

Looking back over our lives to clearly see how we have allowed our fears to shape who we are and the world around us.

Fear is not bias to age, social class, financial status, race, creed, color, nor sexual orientation. It doesn't matter who you are or what you do, you are not exempt from fear. Oftentimes, our fears are created as a result of our childhood experiences; which carries on with us throughout our adulthood. Especially in areas

Empowering Survivors

AFFIRMATION OF PEACE

Peace. Now more than ever, we want to maintain inner peace no matter what is going on around us. Therefore, we should not let fear control our lives.

Affirmation: I am developing the skills and courage to face life with faith rather than fear.

that deal with matters of gravity, world destruction, situations of physical harm/abuse, or imposed fear from others. These haunting reservations become the canvas for the portrait of lives.

Recognize

- *Emotional Fear*
- *Spiritual Fear*
- *Mental Fear*
- *Physical Fear*
- *Social Fear*
- *Worldly Fear*

Fear can bring about a number of "disabling" emotions such as shyness, doubt, isolation and lower our self-esteem. This is why we may tend to feel unfulfilled.

The Bible tells us that fear was not a part of the 'blueprint' that God used when he created us. Considering this, we have to be careful about letting fear hinder our lives.

Release-*Working hard toward overcoming fears.*

By learning to release your fears you can begin to feel free. Take for instance, the fear of public speaking. Many of us may have encountered times of a little *"stage-fright"* when asked to give a speech or do an announcement in front of an audience.

I'll never forget my first time speaking in a public setting, I felt adrenaline race through my body and a panic attack brewing in my spirit. But, as I thought about my speech and the meaning of its purpose God's peace started to overtake me.

Still, as I walked up to the podium I could feel my legs trembling but as I looked out into the audience I felt their warm reception of my cause; which helped me to deliver the message with passion.

> *I've learned to embrace my fears*
> *and I work hard toward overcoming them.*
> *I'm Still Standing*

Compounding Fear

Oftentimes, we perpetuate fear causing it to build up based on our past experiences or based on the opinioned fears of others. Traumatic events such as abuse [verbal, physical or otherwise] can also be a leading cause of compounding fear. However, when we compound our fears—one upon another—we tend to bury our blessings.

> *I am learning to live beyond my fears.*
> *I'm Still Standing*

Finding Your Own Rhythm

"The wisdom of rhythm comes by living in faith and not fear."
–Tamiko Lowry

In my opinion, it is within our fears that we ultimately find our faith and begin to understand the rhythm of our purpose. Though we will always have fears that we may never face, it is within the one's that we choose to conquer [prayerfully] that brings about a testament of survival. As we learn, we grow; ultimately beginning to move forward finding wisdom and purpose for our journey.

My life will no longer be ruled by fear.
I'm Still Standing

Survival Talk-

TOPIC of DISCUSSION:

- *Why do you fear?*
- *What do you fear most?*
- *At what age did you realize your fear?*
- *How do you respond to your fear?*
- *Who or what inspired you to overcome your fear?*

Conquering our fears also help to build courage, so that we can look forward to living in the full blessings of survival.

Chapter Four

DADDY'S GIRL

On my 7th birthday, my dad showed up with a bike—a pink dessert rose Huffy with tassels hanging from the handle bars. From my memory that was the first time my dad had ever bought anything for me. One time, he actually bought me a fur coat. I thought that I was big time Hollywood. It was my favorite coat and if my mom would've let me I would have worn it in the summer time.

I didn't see much of my dad, but whenever he did come around it brought me joy. As little girls we look to our fathers to be that sense of security. The protector, the provider, the King of our fairytale castle. However, because I grew up without my father being in the household, I never knew what security felt like. I never knew what it was like to have the true love of a father or to be *'daddy's little girl'*.

It was around the age of eight when I began to realize that my dad was a pimp and my mom was a prostitute. My aunts [on my dad's side of the family] would ask me what my dad did for a living and I would say, "Pimp them hoes and get that *geech.*" (in my sweet, shy-like tone). Geech was a term used for money in the early 80's. They would crack up laughing and make me repeat it over and over. I think these were the years in which I started to believe that abuse, drugs, and alcohol were normal. Of course, because all of these elements were around me all of the time.

I even recall a time when my aunts were smoking marijuana and blew the smoke in my face to see if I would get high. As I sat there quietly, trying to close my nose to avoid breathing in the thick cloud, they laughed.

Seeing as though I was so timid, I wouldn't talk much. So, I just remained quiet (like always) and didn't say a word while they continued on in their "party mode". But, in my little mind, I really didn't get the point of it all.

Though I began seeing a little more of my dad's family, I still could not connect to his love for me. I remember longing for wanting to be with him; to be in the safety of his presence. My desire to be close to him would make me feel hopeful. Yet, his actions detoured me. Promises made, promises broken. I wondered why he could be so distant and sometimes cold. Maybe he didn't really love me? I thought to myself.

As time went on, I began to accept his distance—eventually creating my own. The way that I witnessed him behave around me, the way he treated women and his nonchalant attitude toward me made me feel dispirited; ultimately looking to others for answers.

"Though I never felt the love of an earthly father, I was wonderfully made, loved, reared and protected by my Heavenly Father."
I'm Still Standing

Fathers are essential to a child's life. It is through the bond of a father that we feel our sense of protection, learn the authority of life, find our comfort and ultimately look to for acceptance or approval. Fathers are creators; creators of the seed of life that forms within our mother's womb. It is here, at the root of our existence that we naturally gravitate toward for life's cultivation.

In most cases, [whether girl or boy] when a child grows up without the presence of a father the child can tend to feel inferior or a sense of lack. *None-the-less* questioning themselves for the actions of the father. Though there are some that do not know of/or have never met their fathers, we all can take comfort in knowing that we have a Heavenly Father that the Bible tells us is a father to the fatherless.

As I take this time to reflect, I understand the effects of not having my father around full-time. I felt as if a piece of my heart was always missing. There were times when I felt angry—broken & hurt wishing for my dad to rescue me. The yearning for a nurturing manly --"daddy's"-- hug often overtook me. However, I also felt the warming comfort of God reassuring me that *he* was really all that I needed to get by.

And call no man your **father** *upon the earth: f or one is your* **Father***, which is in heaven.—Matthew 23:9*

Parenting is not easy. However, understanding that there will be parenting challenges and trials along the way we must do our best to go the distance to provide our children with a safe, balanced, healhthy lifestyle; so that the child has a fair opportunity for a successful life.

The Presence of a Father/Mother helps to give a child ...

- *Sense of Stabilty*
- *Sense of Protection*
- *Sense of Self-Love and Independence*
- *Support*
- *Truth*
- *Honor*
- *Respect*
- *Inspiration*
- *Unconditional Love*
- *Positive Reassurance*
- *Instruction*
- *Communication*
- *Accountablity*
- *Moral Character*

When one or both parties in a relationship have never actually experienced the connection of a mother's or a father's love there may be realtionship challenges. However, if we begin to heal through our pain we can patiently love in spite of our wounded past.
---Patience, Love and Understanding cleanses the wounds.

Survival Talk-

TOPIC of DISCUSSION

The Love of a Father/Mother.

- **Did you grow up with or without a father/mother in the home?**
- **How do you feel it affected you as a child? ...as an adult?**
- **If you currently raising children without a father/mother, how does the situation impact their lives?**
- **If you could change anything about your relationship with your dad/mom...what would it be?**

INTERMISSION for the 'INNERMission'

O ur past gives us an identity.
Our future is shaped by who we
think we are and what we can be.

- Tamiko Lowry

I n the previous chapters
of this book, I have
shared with you the beginning of
my journey. My past experiences
as a child, the meaning of my
name, the generational curses, the
abuse, not having a father figure,
and what brought a smile to my
face. Those small yet, major
incidents in my life that groomed
me to be the person I am today.

So many of us are
wounded throughout our lives that
we tend to forget how we got to
where we are today. We
block out the painful experiences not realizing that that
pain could one day lead to our purpose.

*What are the things in your past that you have blocked
out that are keeping you from reaching your purpose in life?*

Going back to our past and facing it 'head-on' can reveal our true authentic identity.

It wasn't until I learned and studied the meaning of my name that I was able to better understand my journey, and my purpose in life. *Have you ever really studied and learned the meaning of your name?*

The power of a name and its value influences your character. It's what identifies you throughout your life. Take some time to research the meaning of your name and study the characteristics. By doing so you will find out who you authentically are as a person.

TIME OUT:

Taking time to research your name promotes self-awareness. It also helps you to learn your ancestral history to give you insight into [what I call] *'warning wounds'*; events of our past that can cause hindrances within your future—if not careful.

www.tamikolowry.com

Standing in God's Purpose

God will use whatever he wants to display his glory.

A season of suffering is a small assignment when compared to the reward. Your problems, struggles, and pain all have a purpose.

Rather than be angry about the things that you have gone through, explore it. Ponder it. Use it to the glory of God.

We love, we live, we stand...we are Still Standing!"

- Tamiko Lowry

RELATIONSHIP WOE'S

RELATIONS OF LIFE

For as long as I could remember, my mom
always chose 'unhealthy' relationships. The first one
[as I mentioned earlier in the book] was very abusive.
That was the guy that moved us to Washington, DC.
Once she left him, when we came back to Buffalo she
started dating another guy who was a very well-known
"numbers runner". Back in those days, "running
numbers" was a lucrative business. So, most of the time
he carried lots of money.

He was much older than my mom (as were most
of her boyfriends). He lived with us for a short time.
Though I remember them arguing a lot, never recall
him ever hitting her. It was more along the lines of
verbal and emotional abuse. Then, one day he just
disappeared and we never saw him again.

Shortly after that, my mom dated another older
man who owned a bar. From what I could recollect, he
had a wife. But, that didn't seem to matter, seeing as
though he took really good care of us. Although I knew
that he was a married man (that had lots of other

women on the side) surprisingly, I liked him out of all the men that she ever dated.

In between boyfriends my mom and one of her friends would frequently go to New York City to prostitute to make money. I don't believe she was aware that I knew what she was doing; because I was so young and never really commented about a lot of things. But, I was extremely observant.

Eventually, my mom landed a job at a bakery not too far from our house. I was a 'latch key' kid; so I was always home alone. I remember a time that I was home alone and a man tried to come through my bed room window. It frightened me so much that I darted out the door wearing only my pajamas. I ran several blocks to my aunt's house.

It wasn't until the next morning that my mom picked me up from my aunt's house. As I expressed my fear, while telling her what happened I guess I expected her to release some type of compassion. Needless to say, she still beat me because I left her door unlocked.

My aunts would always try to protect me from my mom's crazy outrageous outbursts. As I got older I just got used to my mother's ways. The verbal and physical abuse became normal for me.

During my preteen and teenage years, I began to visit my father who relocated to Atlanta, GA. Seemed like every time I visited him, he would have multiple girlfriends around him. It behooved me that they all thought that they were the main woman. They would do things for me to impress me [*My guess was it made them think that getting me to like them would attract my father*].

This experience, coupled with other examples of relationship woes that I witnessed with my mother all set the tone for my views of the way a man should treat a woman. –Wounded Relationships.

Witnessing the Wounds of the Wounded

Our upbringing can definitely shape world and influence our view of relationships. As we carry these opinions from our wounded experiences along with us into our adulthood, we must be careful not to let them hinder us.

In some instances, we become so overly phobic of events that happened in our lives that we tend to repeat or recreate those same wounded` accounts unconsciously. Take for example, a child that constantly experiences abuse. It is likely that the child will grow to mirror those abusive traits.

Why?...

Over time, through repetition our brain holds images from those 'woundful' situations that we may view to be traumatic. Those events tap into our inner emotion causing us to feel either a sense of acceptance or rejection. If accepted, the child may feel as though it's 'normal' for him/her to recant certain events. While if rejected, the child may see abuse to be wrong and vow never to involve themselves in such acts.

"Have you ever heard someone say that they tried hard not to be like their parents or someone else, then ended up in the same situations or worse?"

This will hold true if we are not aware of our actions. This is why it is vital to your wellness to take time out to get to know your 'inner'self, explore your redesign [if necessary], and discover a 'new' you.

Wounded relationships of my past will not dictate my future relationships (personal or business).
I'm still Standing

Though my opinions were formed by
unfortunate events of my past...

I'm Still Standing

Survival Talk-

TOPIC of DISCUSSION

Family, Social & Business Relations

▣ **What [to you] makes a healthy relationship?**
▣ **How do you currently view your relationships (family/social/business)?**
▣ **Do you feel as though your past has a negative or positive effect in how you relate to others?**
▣ **Do you feel as though you need to redesign your life to experience healthier relationships?**

Awareness...*Power of Loving Yourself*

One of the most powerful lessons that I have learned throughout my life is that loving myself is very key to my happiness and emotional well-being. It is a fact that many people are not even aware of. Love is a powerful force in our lives and can be used to remedy many heartaches & pain. It gives us clarity of mind and motivation to be a better person. It helps us achieve greater things for ourselves—mind, body and spirit.

Love Yourself!

Tamiko Lowry-
Founder of The Still
Standing Foundation

(Photo by Michael Sharp Photography)

Identify various forms of abuse...

There are many forms of Domestic Abuse; some of which we tend to overlook for various reasons such as love, compassion, marital/relationship arrangement, financial dependency, or childhood past. These hurtful, harmful acts causes wounding in our lives—ultimately bringing us to a place of confusion, brokenness or shame.

As an advocate of Survivorship from Abuse, I speak strongly about awareness to help bring to light those aliments in our lives that causes us to become wounded.

The first step is clearly identifying abuse.

Physical
Shoving, hitting, pulling, choking, biting, kicking, abandoning, isolation, head-butting, pinching, slapping, throwing things.

Verbal Abuse
Name calling, insulting, threatening, demeaning, raising tone of voice, profane verbal outburst.

Emotional Abuse
Ignoring, threatening, intimating, using traumatic situations or experiences against you, threating to harm themselves, threating to harm children, friends or family members.

Financial/Economic Abuse-Financially controlling, Stealing from bank/credit card accounts, denial of financial resources, intentional damage to credit, withholding support for children.

Sexual Abuse-Sex by force. Sex without mutual consent.

Over time, as we begin to blame ourselves for the unfortunate behaviors of our offenders we not only suffer from the outer effects, but also the inner pain; which lowers our self-esteem and hinders our growth potential.

Recognizing Dating Violence

In my research, I have found that the mass majority of those in abusive relationships were those that have experienced or witnessed some sort of abuse as a child. Sadly enough, many of those individuals viewed abuse as *"normal"* behavior or some even felt as though being abused was warranted…saying things such as:

> *"If he doesn't hit me that means that he doesn't love me or care."*
>
> *"If he doesn't call me constantly to find out my whereabouts he doesn't care about me."*
>
> *"If she doesn't argue at me, maybe she doesn't care."*
>
> *"As long as he/she pays the bills, I can take it."*

With that being said, relationship abuse has been noted as an on-going epidemic, generation-after-generation based on hurt and continual uninhibited thinking patterns.

Seeing as though I too, have had my share of abuse within relationships, I can grasp ahold of how this can be construed as a plaguing affect. However, for me, it was being able to look back over my experiences, recognizing certain behavior to understand that abuse (verbal, emotional, physical, etc.) should not be a way of life.

As we begin to form our forward opinions of relationships we must be able to identify the difference between a **healthy relationship** and a **toxic relationship;** being mindful and watchful for abusive traits.

Toxic Relationships

- Physically Abusive,
- Verbally Abusive, (outbursts/arguing, name calling, insulting),
- Emotionally Abusive ("Punishing")
- Negatively Persuasive
- Religiously Controlling,
- Isolating (separating from friends and family),
- Sexually Abusive,
- Raging,
- Resentful,
- Threatening,
- Apologetic/Blaming after acts of abuse,
- Forceful with any act without mutual consent.

IDENTIFY

Healthy Relationships

- Loving,
- Complementing,
- Respectful,
- Affectionate,
- Considerate,
- Loyal,
- Trustworthy,
- Encouraging,
- Unconditional,
- Inspiring,
- Pleasurable,
- Compassionate,
- Exemplify Moral Character,
- Easy Going
- Not Forceful

IDENTIFY

Persuasion can be a form of abuse as well; which can be equally compared to controlling. The act of persuasion is usually used to influence or induce us to do things that are generally outside of our 'moral character'. Many times in relationships, persuasion is used in situations that involve, drugs, alcohol sex or religion—all circumstances that can become detrimental to our overall health and wellness.

Persuasive abuse taps into our minds giving way into our inner emotion; which helps our abuser to manipulate us into trying drugs, drinking, having sex with others or steering us into bondage under religion. Some even feel that sex after abuse is a way to persuade you to forgive and forget.

Oftentimes, your partner will be very apologetic after abusive behavior. Attempting to do nice things or buy gifts. There are also times when your partner may become increasingly withdrawn, ignoring or blaming. In my opinion, the saying holds true ....*if your partner uses a form of abuse against you once, they will in fact try it again (in the same or another form)*. Therefore, it is important to consult with a counselor, mentor or other care professional to begin to seek help immediately. Don't wait until it's too late.

Keeping in mind that family members, co-workers or friends may lend an ear, be careful when choosing someone to confide in about the details of your abusive situation. Though they may love or care about you, the truth is everyone is not equipped to offer safe, sound unbiased advice—not to say that they will not support you, just be aware how much you share so that you are clear in making your own choices.

The Will of Survival

Have a Survival Plan—

your life depends on it!

If you are currently experiencing acts of Domestic Abuse it is important to find resources that can help you as you plan to leave the situation.

- Think before you react.

- During an argument try your best to stay calm. Try to avoid arguing in rooms such as the kitchen which has sharp objects or rooms that only have one way in and out like the bathroom.

- Identify a safe place (a friend's house that your mate would not look to find you or hotel (if close to your home, be sure to have the phone number to the hotel security easily accessible).

- Always keep a telephone cellphone, or internet connection capabilities readily available at ALL times. Program your equipment using its voice feature to identify an emergency tone within your voice. Example: Speaking into your device say the following…

"Help"

or

use a 'CODE WORD" so that your phone, tablet or other programmable device calls for help if you are in a stressful situation.

Code words are also good to have to alert children, friends or family members if you find yourself in a position of distress when you're dealing with an abusive partner.

- Be cautious and safe.

- Build a support system.

  Identify at least one-to-two people to confide in that will be of support when you decide to leave or that will be contacts in case of emergency.

- Inform your child's school administrator/childcare provider that your family will be in transition due to an abusive partner. Also noting that potential absences may occur during your transition period so that they are aware. Sometimes they too may be able to offer various alternatives and resources to help.

- Check your company's FMLA/Family Violence Leave Policy for details of terms and compensation information to know rights as well as your benefits, should you need to take time off of work.

- Always keep money, important papers and documentation with you at all times.

- Strategically pack clothing and store in an inconspicuous, yet easily accessible location; so that your partner does not suspect your plan. (This may cause your partner to become frustrated and abusive).

- Learn the route to your safe destination and plan a transportation method if you do not own a car. Always be sure to have access tools like keys or keyless entry devices to vehicle handy.

- Open a PO Box to forward all correspondences. Try to select a Post Office that is easily accessible for you to retrieve your mail; however be sure that it will not reveal your safe place.

  Sometimes we may not be in a position to plan, therefore in all emergency situations its best to call your local authorities or 911 for assistance.

"It takes courage to walk away."

━━━━━━━━━━━━━━━━━━━

Support for Survivors Healing from Abuse

*Finding a great Certified Life Coach to provide prayer,
support and mentorship will help along the way.*

━━━━━━━━━━━━━━━

Areas of Survival Support

- ❑ Assistance with finding safe shelter
- ❑ Assistance locating resources for food, clothing and transportation
- ❑ Employment referrals
- ❑ Educational Resources
- ❑ Training/Vocational Leaning Workshops
- ❑ Health/Fitness workshops
- ❑ Childcare referrals
- ❑ Counseling Groups
- ❑ Bereavement coaching
- ❑ Court chaperone
- ❑ Credit counseling
- ❑ Financial assistance
- ❑ General referrals to agencies and other support organizations

RUNNING FREE

"Running away will never make you free."

Kenny Loggins

When I was fourteen years old, I remember returning home to Buffalo after being with my dad for the summer in Atlanta to find out that my mom found a new boyfriend. They broke the news to me that they were planning to get married. However, I really didn't like the new boyfriend. He didn't have a job nor seem to be a very honest man. Though he and my mom would always argue and bicker. But, they still ended up getting married.

There were times when her 'new husband' would come into my bedroom while I was asleep, just to stand in the doorway there staring at me. On one occasion, he even came in the bathroom while I was in the shower saying that he didn't know I was in there; proclaiming it to be an accident. From that point forward, I was always careful around him as he made me very uncomfortable.

One night, I can also recall getting so angry with him about arguing with my mom, that I grabbed an umbrella [one with a pointy tip] directing it at him; threatening that I would stab him if he didn't leave her alone. Later, I found out that he was addicted to crack cocaine, used heroin and not to mention an uncontrolled alcoholic.

During these years, my mom too, would still dabble in crack cocaine every now-and-then. She was considered to be a functional drug user. Meaning, she would pay her bills and make sure her house was in order, but would spend the rest of the money on drugs. There were times when she would get a hefty income tax return then give me money from it to go shopping or buy things that I needed for school. But, she would go on these crack binges and spend lots of money on the drug. She would then come to me asking for the money that she gave me to buy more drugs.

After all of the back and forth of my mother's 'money roller-coaster rides' I decided that I wanted to get a job so that I could secure my own money. So, I started applying.

Then finally, I was able land a job as a telemarketer. I don't recall how much I made per hour, yet I remember getting my first check for $48. I thought to myself, what am supposed to do with $48?

At the time, I was seeing someone and his birthday was coming up so I wanted to buy him something nice. Since the check was handwritten, I forged the check by putting a number one in front of the forty-eight making the check $148. One of my mom's ex-boyfriend's (the married bar owner) cashed the check for me. Then, a week or so later the check came back saying that it was forged. Instead of taking me to court, my boss fired me and made me pay the money back. Even the bar owner was very upset with me because his involvement caused him a little trouble as well. I remember my mom telling me that I was a thief just like my father.

My mother was always verbally abusive to me; but as I started to get older I didn't like it. One time, I got angry at her so I ran away. I took a $4 Greyhound bus to Rochester, NY…where I knew a friend. I think I stayed there for about four days.

During my stay I smoked marijuana for the first time. I even remember buying a gold tooth with a money sign engraved in it. I thought I was living the good life. After a few days [when I ran out of money] I was ready to go back home. I called my mom to let her know that I was 'OK' and that I ran away because I didn't think she loved me. Her response was warm as said she loved me and wanted me back home so that we could talk it out.

Then, as soon as I got home I remember her snatching me in the house. She had an iron in her hand and acted as if she was going to burn me with it. When she noticed the gold tooth in my mouth, she held me up against the wall; grabbing me by the throat, snatching the tooth out of my mouth. I knew at that point that nothing changed.

I ran away several times during my teenage years hoping to get my mom's attention—but it didn't work. I don't think my mom realized that she was mentally abusing me. She would call me names and tell me that I was stupid.

On several occasions she told me that she wishes that she would have never had me and that she should have aborted me. She told me this many times throughout life. Those words pierced my soul for years.

Verbal wounds did not break me.
I'm Still Standing

As a child, I remember reciting a
nursery rhyme...
"Sticks and stones may break my bones,
but words will never hurt me."

Author Unknown

Verbal abuse hurts just the same,
if not worse than physical abuse.

{Stand Against Verbal Abuse}

TIME OUT:

Taking time to celebrate yourself for all that you are [a great creation of God] will help to combat the negative words that others try to speak into your life. If you constantly affirm to yourself who you are and what you are…that is ultimately what you will become.

Do not let the opinions of others (family, business associates or friends) overshadow the beauty that you possess inside and out.

www.tamikolowry.com

Chapter Seven

MATTERS OF THE
MIND, HEART & SPIRIT

"If I knew then, what I know now I…"-Wisdom

A Teenage Love,
Babies having Babies

During the summer before my junior year of high school, I met a young man who was a star football and basketball player. He would buy me expensive sneakers and clothes; things that my mom couldn't afford. He was also a local drug dealer, so he had more money than the *average* teenage boy. I felt like I was on top of the world dating him. I would wear his football jersey to school and all the other girls were jealous of me.

He was my first 'real' boyfriend. I felt a sense of security when we were together. I think it was due to the fact that I didn't really have my father around. Therefore, having a boyfriend to care for and take care of me made me feel special. The first time that we had sex, I got pregnant. I was afraid to tell my mom, so I snuck to get an abortion.

After the abortion I got really sick. Apparently, I had an allergic reaction to some medication and it caused my body to mimic a stroke. I thought for sure that I was dying.

My mom didn't know what was wrong with me so she called the ambulance. I got to the emergency room and they ran several tests that indicated that I was having an allergic reaction to the medication that I was on. They also ran a pregnancy test that came back positive. My mom kept arguing with the doctor saying that I was a virgin and there was no way that I could be pregnant. It was at that time that I had to confess to my mom that I had just gotten an abortion a few days earlier which is why the pregnancy test kept coming back positive. Then a week or so later, a letter came in the mail saying that my test results came back stating that I had an STD.

Here, in less than a month I had gotten pregnant, an abortion and contracted an STD. My boyfriend told me that he caught the disease from someone who he slept with before me. So, the both of us got treated and remained in the relationship. But, later I found out that he'd been cheating on me with several girls.

After a while he started to get very jealous and possessive. If I tried to break up with him, he would always threaten to kill himself. Consequently, I stayed with him because I felt sorry for him. A few months later I got pregnant *again*. Only this time, I did not want to get another abortion; so I decided to have the baby.

In 1992, my junior year of high school I gave birth to a beautiful baby girl—at the age of 17. I became a mother. While before I got pregnant, I was preparing for the Miss Teen USA pageant. However, I had to step down from the pageant. The hardest part was telling my aunt and those in the community who financially sponsored me for the pageant about my pregnancy.

I often think about my uncle who used to always tell me that I was going to be the next Miss Black America. A part of me felt like I failed them. I was smart and got good grades so my family had high expectations of me. However, when I became pregnant their opinions changed.

Moving Forward
In Spite of Challenges

My senior year of high school I was sent to a special school for teenage mothers. The school even had a daycare onsite. So everyday my daughter was able to come to school with me. In addition to our regular school work we also required to attend parenting classes to prepare us for parenthood.

In June of 1993, I walked across the stage at Kleinhans Music Hall to receive my high school diploma. My daughter [who was almost a year old] sat in the audience with my mom and other family members cheering me on. Unlike many teenage moms, I decided to finish high school. Later, enrolling in college the following semester.

In theory and in truth, I was a considered to be a statistic—because I was a teenage mom. With this in mind, I did not want to become a high school dropout as well. So, I stayed focused and determined.

I wanted to reap the harvest of my hard labor and prove to my family that I was not a failure. I loved myself enough to understand the love of the mother— with the ultimate sacrifice for my child [whom I now needed to set a good example for].

Now, the day has come that I stand with others to unite in a journey far beyond what my mind would have imagined back at that time. God's plan is amazing!

I strive to move forward in spite of my challenges.
I'm Still Standing

Goal setting and proper planning will help you to move forward with your life goals [mind, body and spirit].

Goal setting is vital to your growth and wellness!

If you don't know where you are going, *how will you ever know when you get there?*

As you begin to take time to consider your future, writing or journaling each goal will help you to begin to see the vision. Then, once the vision is realized you will begin to take action to manifest it.

Vision takes confidence.

Planning requires action.

In the bible outlines that faith without works is dead
—James 2:14-26.

Moving forward in a greater direction should always encourage us to reach higher. Just think of learning to ride a bicycle. Initially, there is a vision which is followed by an action. Though there is a chance that you may fall—becoming wounded—you can still build up enough courage to try it until you have achieved.

[Wounds to Wisdom...I'm Still Standing]

AFFIRMATION

Today, I will plan my goals and take action so that I reach my next level.

Visualize your plan and put it in action —

your life depends on it.

Survival Talk-

TOPIC of DISCUSSION

Moving forward with goals (educational goals, career goals, spiritual goals, etc.) in spite of the past & the negative comments/actions of others.

- *What are your goals?*
- *What are you plans for achieving your goals?*
- *What are the challenges that you feel may interfere with the achievement of your goals?*
- *How will you celebrate your accomplishment?*

Wounded by Loss

My best friend dated a local drug dealer whom was *very* abusive to her. He would beat her up and cuss her out, choke her and use other scare tactics to make her feel fearful and intimidated. Looking back just gives me chills, and it hurts to know that there were many all-around the world experiencing the same or similar acts of abuse. Some bragged about it; saying *"If a man doesn't hit you then he must not care about you or love you."* Others tried hard to hide the abuse by covering up the scars, yet it didn't take long before the wound told the story.

When she first start dating him things seemed to be going well for them. However, as time progressed his 'true colors' revealed themselves. He began controlling her every move. Eager to make him happy she began to miss class on a regular basis to be with him. One day, she did not come to school at all. Her mom was calling around looking for her. A few hours later we found out that she had been shot in the head and killed by her boyfriend. She was also pregnant at the time. My heart deeply ached for her family.

I was distraught for a very long time. This was one of my dearest and closest friends. There were so many times when my daughter's father would threaten to kill me if I left him too. I thought to myself how that could have been me. I considered myself lucky.

-Rest in Peace, Michelle

Survival Talk-

TOPIC of DISCUSSION

Loss/Finding a Bereavement Coach

Losing someone that is near and dear to us due to an abusive situation can be quite unnerving and upsetting. The feelings that flow through our emotional stream can also conjure up rant, rage, resentment, unforgiveness, etc. However, we must remember that just as we are forgiven, we too must forgive.

- *Have you ever lost a loved one, coworker or friend due abuse?*
- *Did you have support to help you morn your loss?*
- *How did the loss impact how you view abuse today?*

Did you Know?

Statistics reveal that 1 out of 3 of all female homicide victims are killed by a current of former intimate partner.

National Domestic Violence Resource Center

The Spiritual Search

Wounds of the Spirit

After I graduated, I immediately moved out of my mom's house. I wanted to feel like an adult—feel a sense of freedom. Then, a few months later I decided I wanted to convert to practicing Islam. I guess I was searching for something...just didn't know what it was.

During that time, studying under the Islamic teachings of a powerful organization became very popular for young Blacks in the 90's; so, I joined. Shortly after attending the Mosque, I began a courtship with one of the brothers. *The rule* was that we were supposed to be married after twelve weeks of courtship. Although I cared for him very much, I felt controlled.

I remember feeling forced into marriage based on the laws, principles and practices of the organization. Here, I was only eighteen or nineteen years old in search of freedom choosing a life of bondage. The control dictated everything that I ate, drank [...] what I wore and where I went.

I wanted to be free. I wanted to party wearing short dresses or miniskirts. Of course that would have been a *'no-no'* in the community. Needless to say, I eventually left the mosque and broke up with the brother that I was supposed to marry. He was heartbroken.

I became a party girl...

I began to go out more frequently—attending all of the parties. So, I became very popular on the college campus. The brother from the organization that I was supposed to marry went to the same college as well; which didn't make it a good situation for me. He began stalking me; begging for me to take him back. At this point, I wanted nothing to do with him or the mosque. I felt like I was experiencing the most freedom that I ever had in my life.

I would party every weekend, leaving my daughter with my mom and other family members. Over time I ended up spending my time with someone who I felt interested in dating. In the beginning he treated me very well. Funny, but we had a connection as friends for many years because our fathers were good friends.

After a while he too, became very possessive and promiscuous. Little did I know, I was entertaining another emotionally abusive relationship. Eventually, I got tired of his possessiveness; likewise the cheating. So, I tried to break off the relationship.

When I communicated to him that I no longer wanted to be in the relationship with him he lunged at me; choked me [...] then yanked me throughout the house by my hair. I yelled, kicked and screamed for him to let me go. All while crying out to God to save me from the grips of his fingers.

My body began to feel numb, as he yanked me into the bathroom with his hands firmly secured around my neck (choking me uncontrollably). Did I mention that during all of this, he's telling me that he loves me? Basically, begging me to stay with him. Afterward he spent his time trying to apologize for hurting me. But, I did not get caught in his 'web'; I broke up with him—never to be bothered with him again.

Survival Talk-

TOPIC *of* DISCUSSION

Feeling Free

- 📢 ***What makes you feel free?***
- 📢 ***What makes you feel controlled?***
- 📢 ***Do you have feeling of rebellion when you feel that you want to be free?***

The Shock and Bondage of Sexual Assault

While in my early twenties, I befriended a few individuals that I considered to be trustworthy to hang out with. Needless to say, we became a close-knit group. Most weekends we hung out at events and nightclubs around town together.

However, there was one particular guy that I viewed as more of a brother. As time went on, he and I became very close. He always seemed to be responsible and I felt very safe around him.

One night, my female cousin, he and I decided to go to a night club [assigning him as the designated driver]. Nothing really seemed to be unusual about the night; we had a few drinks, danced, laughed—basically having a great time like always.

When we left the club, he drove my cousin home first. Then, not soon after dropping her off, my "so called" friend began to rub his hand up and down my leg; which made me very uncomfortable.

So, I asked him to stop. He refused…and proceeded to forcefully rub my leg. I cringed and resisted as his hand moved closer to my vaginal area.

I kept demanding him again to *stop* while pushing his hand away. Then, he abruptly pulled the car over.

Once the car stopped, I got out…attempting to run. However, he quickly burst out of the driver's side of the car, running toward me. As he got closer to me I felt my heart race. Then, he grabbed me so tightly that I could not breathe. I tried my best to scream. But of course, no one heard me because it was three o'clock in the morning. There was no one was out and we were parked in a back alley.

He was much stronger so it was very difficult to try to fight him off. He threw me in the back seat of the car. We tussled and fought for was seemed like a really long time. My heart, my body and my mind eventually got tired, and I gave up fighting.

Although he did not penetrate me with his penis, he used his fist to shove it up my vagina several times; physically hurting me. He then performed oral sex on me. The entire time, I cried while asking him why he was doing this to me. His answer was… *"Maybe you shouldn't be so damn pretty."*

So, for a few years following that incident, I downplayed my looks. I wore baseball hats, baggy jeans and wouldn't groom myself. I thought that if I looked too pretty that it would happen to me again. I didn't want be the pretty girl anymore.

This incident along with all the other unhealthy circumstances around me made me want to leave Buffalo—for good. I wanted to forget all those horrible things that happened to me. So, I decided that by moving to Atlanta I could get a fresh start.

Though my cries fell on deaf ears and my pain felt unbearable, God fought my battle so that I would be set free, healed and delivered.

I'm Still Standing

Sexual Assault is a physically aggressive or mind manipulating act that hurts an individual physically and emotionally. It is one of the world's most unreported attacks; unbiased to woman or men. Oftentimes sexual abuse leaves the victim feeling as though their attack was a warranted based on something that they did, they wore or how they carried themselves—which is unfortunate, sad and untrue.

The unnerving experience of sexual assault can leave one in bondage; tortured by the evil ailments of its occurrence.

Primarily, the remembrance of the event also commits an individual to searching for answers as to "Why…or Why me?" creating a sense of demoralizing fear. This sets the tone for other hindering factors to infiltrate our thought process and place a negative effect on our overall wellness.

Sexual assault also causes low self-esteem, withdrawal and affect the way one perceives relations with others moving forward. This is why it is important to seek counseling or psychological help if you have ever experienced such an offense.

Life after sexual assault begins with forgiveness; and though this may be difficult it is necessary. Secondly, you must surround yourself with positive people who exude positive energy; which in all essence helps to promote healing and deliverance.

In an upcoming series, I will talk more in depth about Sexual Abuse and living life bound by sexual warfare. This topic is one that plagues many all over the world (young and old). It has become a major contributing factor that hinders us from living life to our full potential if left unreported & untreated.

Sex should always be consensual.
It should never be forced.

Did you Know?

Experiencing sexual assault can change one's perception of themselves. Thus causing a breakdown in self-esteem and leads to emotional bondage.

It also can affect the way an individual perceives relationships; causing them to become fearful and/or withdrawn.

The Still Standing Foundation research study, Tamiko Lowry

Survival Talk-

TOPIC *of* DISCUSSION

Sexual Assault/Sexual Abuse

- *Have you ever experienced acts of sexual abuse/assault?*
- *How did it make you feel...physically, emotionally?*
- *Have you forgiven your offender?*
- *How has being sexually assaulted affected your past/present relationships?*
- *What methods have you taken to heal from your traumatic experience?*
- *How do you currently view sex in general?*
- *Do you still find yourself blaming yourself for the attack?*

Searching for a New Start
1994

There was so much going on in my life that I felt need to get away from my environment. I wanted to leave the chaos in Buffalo behind. So, I decided to pack up my things and moved to Atlanta. I looked forward to starting a new life. Seeing as though my dad lived there, I planned to stay with him for a few months until I found a job and an apartment. But, living under the same roof with my dad, quickly revealed that he was using drugs heavily.

One night, I came home only to find my dad and some of his friends in the living room smoking crack. I instantly ran into my bedroom to check for my stash of money (the money that I brought with me to pay for an apartment); needless to say it was gone!

At that moment, I knew that my dad or one of his friends took the cash to use it to for drugs. I was so hurt and disappointed. My world felt like it was going to crash!

Frustratingly disgusted, I left my dad's house. I moved in with one of his girlfriends' for a short time— eventually moving back to Buffalo to try and save up again.

Not long after moving back to Buffalo, I met someone. He seemed to be such a gentlemen. Nice, compassionate and kind. Not like the other guys that I dated in the past. He actually had a *decent* job and knew how to treat a lady. I enjoyed our time together by making the best of every moment. He swept me off my feet. I felt it could be love.

As our relationship progressed, we talked more about marriage plans; which included relocating to Atlanta together. Little did I know, God had his plans for us as well? Turns out, I was pregnant. I thought for sure that he would be happy. After all, we were discussing marriage and starting a family anyway—right? In my mind I believed that we would get married, move to Atlanta [...] and live happily ever after.

Just before giving birth to my son, he came to me one afternoon with a heavy heart expressing that he met another woman (that he felt he *"fell in love with"*). Undeniably, he had been cheating on me with her; but leading to believe that *'it just happened'* all of a sudden. Nights I cried, my days were long; I felt as if my heart was ripped from my body and completely smashed.

Certainly, it became a difficult time for me. Downright stressful to say the least. I was devastated. How was I going to move forward with another baby alone? Though the situation proved to be quite a nerve-wracking, my handsome baby boy became the best gift.

A few months after our son was born he left for Atlanta with his new girlfriend with no regard for his son & me—subsequently a year later he married her. Ultimately, the part that hurt me the most was that they got married on our son's first birthday. This was the first and only time in my life that my heart had been crushed. I was beyond hurt. This was supposed to be my *Prince Charming*, my *'Knight in shining armor'*. It was then that my 'wall of resistance' went up. At that point, I didn't think I would ever be able to give love freely ever again.

Though I may experience hurt,

> *I know that I was created to love.*
>> *I'm Still Standing*

When the things seem to be against you,
take comfort in knowing that
God is ALWAYS with you.

Chapter Eight

BELIEVING IN
HEALING & DELIVERANCE

"When I cried out for help, *you* answered me.
You made me bold and energized me."
Psalms 138:3

(1996)

During the pregnancy with my son, a sonogram revealed that there were tumors all over his brain. According to the diagnosis, he would have Down-Syndrome. So, the doctors recommended that I have an abortion. I could not believe what I was hearing. I never did drugs and lived a very healthy lifestyle. *Why was this happening to my baby?* I refused to listen to the doctors. I knew in my heart that God would have the final word; so I went home and prayed.

My aunt came to get me and took me to church. There, we prayed for a miracle. She laid hands on my stomach praying; declaring a healing over my son. On my next visit to the doctor for my follow up, astoundingly they could not find the tumors anywhere on his brain. The sonogram came back clean.

They could not believe their eyes. I knew my baby was going to be OK. God heard my cry granting his favor and mercy to my prayers. *He* works miracles.

These days my son is doing very well. He has always been an honor student even making his way through advanced and gifted classes. When he was in 7th grade, he took his first SAT (a national standardized test used for assessment prior to college admission) scoring higher than most high school students. Forget what the doctors say. *God always has the final answer.*

I believe in God's favor, healing and deliverance.
I'm Still Standing

A month after the birth of my son, I received a phone call from my cousin telling me that my mom was in the hospital, she had been shot and that she might not make it. My mom was on and off of drugs for the past ten years. This particular night, when she went out to get drugs the drug dealer that she was purchasing the drugs from was being robbed. Suddenly, she saw the gun and began to run, but not soon enough.

Apparently, the bullet went through his arm hitting my mom in her upper back piercing her lung and causing it to collapse. When I got to the hospital they told me that my mom died and came back. I'm sure, this was indeed a wakeup call for her. Thankfully she lived to share her testimony.

So much happened in the past year. I fell in love, had a baby, got my heart hurt, and almost lost my mom. *Why me?* I felt like my soul is just wounded. Because I was so wounded and hurt, I did not know how to channel my energy so over the course of the next two years I began to party even more; hanging out with the wrong crowd.

I started drinking and doing God knows what. Some nights, I would end up fighting in the nightclubs consequently get kicked out. One time, my friends and I got into a confrontation at a restaurant.

Once we were seated the trouble maker girls from the club came in. They walked past our table intentionally knocking over our food and calling us names. I told one of the girls that if she called me out my name one more time that I was going to kick her *ass*. So she walked passed my table yelling "B…." I immediately jumped over the table and began to beat the girl up, punching her in her face.

As I looked up I saw my other friend fighting one of the other girls. Before I knew it, I had gotten hit in the head with a syrup bottle. Blood began to rush down my heck. At that point, some guys broke up the fight—and I was rushed to the hospital. I was treated for minor injuries.

That next morning, I was getting baptized at church. I never went to sleep that night. After leaving the hospital I went home to get cleaned up and went directly to church. I remember getting baptized that day but nothing about my lifestyle had really changed. I was angry, and hurt and was not ready to make a change in my life.

I eventually began dating one of the top local drug dealers who took care of me. He paid my bills, bought me nice clothes, bought me a car, and took care of my children. I thought I was living the good life. We would party together, get high, drink, go to concerts, and nice restaurants. I knew he had other women on the side. But, I didn't care. As long as he took care of me.

I remember one of my older female relatives telling me that having a piece of man is better than having no man at all. Especially if he was taking care of me. The one thing that bothered me about this relationship is that he knew that my mom was on drugs. His workers would sell crack to my mom and then report back to us what was happening. Deep down inside I felt bad for dating the guy that would supply my mom's drug habit.

After a few years, I began to grow tired of the lifestyle. I wanted more for myself and my children; and dating drug dealers was not cutting it for me anymore. I knew that there had to be a better way of life. I decided that at the end of the year I was going to make the move to Atlanta again. So, I broke up with my drug dealer boyfriend and got a part-time job at a night club as a waitress.

I worked full time during the day for a major corporate company as customer service professional. My plan was to save up all of my tips as well as the money that I made from my day job to use for my move to Atlanta.

One day, when I came home from work, I looked under my mattress to find that my savings had been stolen. I later found out that it was the maintenance man. All of my savings had been taken *again*. Still, I was determined to get out of the Buffalo. I packed up my 1988 Buick Park Avenue with as much stuff as I could, then headed to Atlanta in October of 1998 to start my new life.

Though I may backslide, I am reminded that
I can pull it back together to move forward.
I'm Still Standing

Survival Wellness...

Prayer

Healing

Forgiveness

Deliverance

(Photo by Michael Sharp Photography)

Affirmations of Wellness

I am healed, delivered and set free!

I am well in my mind, body and spirit.

Positivity is all around me helping me to reach my next level.

I'm Still Standing

Chapter Nine

ATLANTA or BUST

"Failure is the opportunity to begin again more intelligently."
Henry Ford

In October of 1998, I decided to give Atlanta, GA another try. I was tired of living in Buffalo seeing friends die, go to jail or get strung out on drugs. During this time, people from all over the country were relocating to Atlanta—it had a reputation for being the "Black Mecca".

This was a new environment that I had to get used to. African Americans were doing well in Atlanta. What was funny to me was the fact that I never really seen a man where a suit or tie unless he was going to a funeral. But, here in the A-T-L nice looking guys in suits were everywhere.

In my old environment most guys were into selling drugs or worked at factories. The women in Atlanta were a lot different from what I was used to as well. They were '*extra done up*'. Long hair weaves, colorful fingernails, eyelashes and a face full of Mac Cosmetics makeup. People would look at me and immediately know that I wasn't a Georgia native. I kept it very simple. Bob hairstyle, French Manicure and very little or no makeup. I was considered to be an "around the way" home girl.

My first year living in Atlanta was not easy; yet I was determined not to go back to Buffalo. Initially, I lived with my cousin for a few months before getting my own one bedroom apartment that I shared with my two children. Though I struggled to pay the bills with a small weekly paycheck from my temp agency job. Good news was, I made ends meet and kept food on the table. I thought to myself, maybe when income tax time came, I would be able to pay my bills up for a few months. I was determined not to move back to Buffalo.

In January of 1999, I went to file my income taxes. I was excited because I knew I would have a pretty good refund. The past three months had been financially challenging, so I was looking forward to receiving my income tax check for some added financial relief. I intended to pay my rent up for a few months, catch on payment with my babysitter, and put the rest away in savings.

A few days after filing my taxes, I received a call from the IRS saying that I was not able to claim my children on my taxes because their social security numbers were already used by someone else.

I was confused. *Who would do something like this to me?* I was alone in a big city with no money and no one to turn to for help. A few months later, I found out that it was my dad who had used my children's social security numbers on his taxes. *What type of man would do this to his daughter and grandchildren?*

Our relationship was already not so good from when he stole money from me a few years prior. *Now this?* Fathers are supposed to love and protect their children, not hurt and steal from them! Needless to say, all he did was apologize for what he did. He never returned the money. I didn't speak to him for another four years.

During this time I was working for a temp agency until I was able to find fulltime employment. Then, I finally received a call for an interview.

Obstacle...I did not have a baby sitter to watch my children while I went for the interview. Surely, I did not want to leave them home alone; so I took them to the interview with me. At that time Destiny was seven years old and Michael was three.

Hoping that the interview didn't take long I left them in the car while I went in for the interview. Rational...It was either go to the interview and leave them in the car; or let another job opportunity pass me by and keep on struggling.

The interview took about 45 minutes. When I got back to the car I heard a loud scream coming from my son. I was so afraid!

I raced to the car to find that he had a hair clip stuck in the inside of his jaw. The sharp teeth from the hair clip were biting down on his jaw causing him to be in pain. I slowly removed the clip from his mouth and comforted him until he stopped crying. I was so afraid that someone had seen them in the car alone and would call the police. Thankfully no saw them.

On another occasion, there was a one day temp assignment from the temp agency that I really needed to take, but did not have a babysitter. Since the assignment was right down the street from my house, I decided to take the job thinking it would be *'okay'* to leave the children at home. I figured that I could come to check on them during my lunch break. Though I was very afraid and hesitant about doing it, I also needed to work because I was low on cash.

I told my children that I was going to leave for a little while instructing them not to answer the door and that I would be back to check on them.

During my lunch break I came home to find them safe and sound. I fed them lunch before heading back to work and also reminded them not to answer the door while I was away. At the time, I didn't have a cell phone so I gave them the number to the front desk.

As I sat in there impatiently rolling back and forth in my chair waiting for my shift to end I worried. Then, as the clock struck 4:59 [four fifty nine] I darted from my chair, grabbed my purse and off I went to check on my babies.

Sad to say, but when I made it home from work that day, my children were not in the house. I was so completely devastated that I began to panic and cry hysterically.

I went outside and there I seen the lady from the leasing office who told me that a representative from the State Childrens' Service Agency came to my apartment to take my babies away because they were home alone. This was indeed one of the worst days of my life. *Why did I leave my babies home alone?*... is all I kept asking myself.

For three long days I was not allowed to see my children. These were the hardest three days of my life. When I went to court I was required to bring a character reference with me—so, I asked my cousin to accompany me.

Seeing as though I did not have a history of child abuse, I was allowed to get my babies back the next day. The looks on their faces when they ran into my arms were *priceless*. They said that they didn't know if they would ever see me again. During those three days, they were placed in a house with several other children who told them that they hadn't seen their parents in years. Needless to say, like so many other single mothers out there I made a decision that could have kept me from ever seeing my children again in life. I prayed and thanked God that I was able to get them back in such a short period of time.

I've learned that my decisions can be costly; I am grateful for God's mercy.
I'm Still Standing

As time went on my situation began to get somewhat better. By the year 2000, I felt stable because I secured two jobs. I worked a full-time job during the day and a part-time as a cocktail waitress at a local strip club at night. Although I never danced at the club, I became friends with many of the dancers. Many of them turned to sex, drugs, and alcohol as a way to cope with their lifestyle. I saw a lot of horrible things happen to these women.

It got to a point to where I could no longer work as the establishment as a waitress. Seeing the way men would treat women and the way the women allowed themselves to be treated like sex objects just didn't sit well with me. So, I quit after a month. I enjoyed having that extra income coming in and I was good at being a cocktail waitress so I decided to get a job at one of the hottest night clubs in the city of Atlanta. They like my personality and gave me a job as a cocktail waitress working in the VIP area.

All of the waitresses wanted to work the VIP section because you were guaranteed to make lots of money in a single night. Celebrities, high rollers and business professionals would spend thousands of dollars on any given night just to sit in VIP—and they tipped us waitresses very well.

The money got so good to me that I ended up quitting my day job. I know bad choice. But by quitting my day job it allowed me to spend more time with my children. I could cook breakfast, drop them off at school, do their homework with them and have a hot meal prepared. I thought that I had the perfect life. I was making good money working as a cocktail waitress in a popular night club, and I was able to be a full-time mom—just like the housewives in the movies.

After a few months of working as a cocktail waitress most of the local celebrities, and high rollers got to know me. They would always request that I be their waiter for the night.

One night, a celebrity guy celebrating his birthday got very intoxicated. He started to rub his hands on my thigh then blatantly said to me

"If you go home with me I will pay your bills for the month." Needless to say, I rejected his offer; telling him that he should go to the strip club if he was looking for a *'cheap whore'*.

I must have embarrassed him because he grabbed me by the arm and pulled me down on the couch next to him. He grabbed my face squeezing my cheeks very hard and told me that if I ever embarrassed him again he would kick my ass. I sat on that couch with tears streaming down my face.

When the manager of the establishment came over I told him what happened. His response to me regarding the situation was...

"If you want to keep your job, keep my VIP clients happy!"

Then he instructed me to take a five minute break to wipe my tears and get myself together. I went to my locker grabbed my belongings and never went back. A few weeks later, I saw on the news that my replacement was raped by a club patron and later died in a fatal car accident trying to get away.

So now I'm back to square one. No job and bills to pay. I started back working for the Temporary Job Agency until I could find another permanent job. While I was working at the nightclub I met a guy that I began to spend lots of time with. We became very close. I eventually introduced him to my children.

About three months into the relationship, I was still working as a temp and barely making enough money to make ends meet. Consequently, I received an eviction notice. So, my boyfriend suggested that I move in with him until I was able to get back on my feet. I thought it would be a great idea as well.

Once I moved in, things seemed to be going great. I even went to his hometown to meet his family. I eventually found a job and began to save so that I could get a new place of my own. When I got ready to start looking for a place to live, my boyfriend suggested that I stay with him a while longer.

Shacking up was something I absolutely did not want to do. Plus, deep down inside I felt that he was not the one. I thanked him for allowing me and my children to stay with him until I got on my feet. I even promised to pay him for the few months that I stayed with him.

He confessed how much he loved me and begged me to stay. I told him that we should just be friends and that I really wanted to get my own place. He got furious and started yelling at me.

He then went to the bedroom and pulled out a gun, he told me that he would kill himself if I left him. I took my children and we hid in the bathroom for about 5 hours until I heard him leave the house. When I knew that he was gone for sure, I grabbed as many as my belongings as I could and we went to my friend's house for safety. He called me for days saying how sorry he was and professing his love for me. We met in person a few weeks later so that I could get the rest of my belongings and he asked me to marry him. I said no and ceased all contact with him.

I finally got my own place and once again things were back to normal. For the next year I focused on work and my children. Once in a while my friends and I would go out to get our party on. Atlanta was known for the hot spots.

One of my friends was celebrating her birthday and decided to get a limo to take us out on the town. We had drank, danced and partied like rock stars that night. This fun night turned tragic. The limo driver proceeded to take us home. When pulled up to the birthday girl's house before the limo driver got out to open the door, I saw a guy run pass the limo with a gun.

I told everyone to duck down because someone had a gun and was pointing it at the limo. I immediately dove to the floor and before I knew it, I heard rounds of shots being fired. We had no idea why this was happening. All I could hear were the screams of my friends and each of them got shot in different parts of their bodies. I thought we were going to die that night.

Once the gun shots stopped we all laid there quiet unsure if it was safe to get up or not. I could hear people saying I've been shot, I'm bleeding. The limo driver lost his arm, one of my friend's arms was severed from a gun wound, and my other friend was shot in the finger. There were a few other passengers who were also injured as a result of the shooting.

By the grace of God, I was not injured. I walked away with only shattered glass in my hair. A few days after this incident rumors began to surface that the shooting was meant for a local rapper who had an altercation with someone just a week earlier. The police said that this was just a case of mistaken identity.

After the shooting incident life was good until I met a guy at a local department store. I would see him every time I went to this particular store. He worked there part-time. He would always compliment me and ask me out on dates and I always declined.

Finally, I decided to give him a chance. We dated for about three months before he proposed to me. *I said yes.* Things were going well in the beginning. We were attending church together every Sunday. He joined the ministerial team at church and I became a Sunday school teacher. We seemed to have it together.

However, my fiancé became very possessive all of a sudden. He would accuse me of cheating on him with any man that spoke to me. If I would hug one of the brothers at church he would accuse me of sleeping with them. His insecurities and possessiveness began to wear me down. More importantly, my children confessed to me that they did not like him. So, I decided to break off the engagement two months before the wedding.

He continued to stalk me for a few months after the breakup. It became such a nuisance that I had to obtain a restraining order from him. Once I broke off this engagement my friends began to call me *"The runaway bride"* because this was the 2nd guy in recent years that had proposed to me.

God will reveal the answers over time.
I'm Still Standing

Chapter Ten

LOOKING FOR LOVE
IN ALL THE WRONG PLACES

"Sometimes we tend to look for things in people, places & things that we think we are lacking, but all we need lies within."
-Tamiko Lowry

A few of my coworkers that were excitingly successful at finding great dates on a new Online Dating website insisted that I should try it out. They boasted about dates with nice men that led to great relationships; and ultimately to marriage. So, I decided to give it a try. So, I set up my Dating Profile Page.

Then, about an hour later I received my first message from a guy. We chatted for a few days online before exchanging phone numbers. After talking on the phone and getting to know each other I found out that he worked with one of my best friends. So I decided to give her a call to inquire about him.

When asked she said *"Girl, he is your type."* Sealing the deal for the date, she went on to say that he was a nice guy, highlighting the good qualities that she knew of him. At first, I was kind of paranoid and apprehensive about going out with someone that I met online. But, since I got the *'OK'* from my friend I felt that I was safe.

We went on our first date, and we immediately *'hit it off'*. Our first date was at a local chain restaurant. There was no seating available so we sat at the bar and talked for hours. He complimented me on my smile, my personality going on to say that he never met anyone like me. He let me know that he was looking for something serious; basically he really wanted to settle down.

Of course, I was very impressed with how well the date went. As soon as I got home I deleted my Dating Profile Account. I thought for sure I met the man of my dreams.

Over the course of the next few months we dated and got to know one another. He met my children and I met his. We became inseparable. Spending all of our free time together. We did family outings with our children. We were becoming a 'real family'.

Though enjoying the moment, things were really moving fast. About four months into the relationship we were having a general conversation when he looked over and said to me "Let's get married." Not too shocked by the question because of how good things were going, I said "OK".

There was no formal engagement. We just agreed that we both wanted to get married. So, we started planning our wedding immediately. I could not believe that I had finally met the man of my dreams. He was very family oriented, a provider, hard-worker, and just adored me. He took on the responsibility of being a father to my children without even thinking twice about it. We became a family in less than a years' time.

Happy, yet still playing in the back of mind were the times during the course of planning the wedding when I noticed that he would get angry and raise his voice at me. There were even times when he would talk to my children in a tone that I didn't like. But, I *'swept it under the rug'* as him being stressed out because of the wedding plans and all of the changes that were taking place in our lives.

A few months before the wedding we decided to start looking for a home that would accommodate our blended family. His children lived out of state but they would visit us every other weekend and during certain holidays. He was very adamant making sure that we got the house that I liked. He wanted to make sure that I was happy and satisfied.

Finally, we decided on a nice four bedroom home. We moved into the house three months before our wedding. I was indeed happy. I had my home, my family, and I was getting married for the first time in my life. Although I had been proposed to several times in the past, I was finally going to do it this time.

Two days after we moved into our new home, my fiancés dad his sister and her three children came to visit; and never left. Here, I just moved into my new home and now it was being *invaded* by strange people. I never let my fiancé know how I felt about his family moving in with us. I thought that as his soon to be wife I should just accept it.

Our household immediately became chaotic. My fiancé began to talk to me as if I were one of the kids. He would yell at the children for no reason. He became very hostile and angry—*all the time*. His *once loving tone of voice* turned harsh and brash.

What did I get myself into?

Excuses...Excuses

He upsettingly became so mean that I didn't want my children around him. Disturbed yet enabling, I justified and attributed his behavior to his sister and her children were living with us. Not to mention the stress from wedding planning. I just hoped that once they found their own place that things would get back to normal. Seeing as though my fiancés rage began to be unbearable, I decided to send my children to Buffalo until the wedding. I felt as though it would relieve a little bit of the pressure.

However, the emotional and verbal outbursts began to get worse after my children left. He would walk around the house and not speak to me for days at a time. In the morning we would be getting dressed for work and he wouldn't speak to me or even say 'good morning'. Then, when I would say good morning to him and he would just look at me and roll his eyes.

At the time, we worked for the same company. Therefore, we drove to work together every day. The drives to work seemed long and dauntingly uncomfortable. He began acting withdrawn, eerie and shared no regard for speaking to me in a very cold manner. Every night he would lock himself in our office room and stay on the computer all night long. I later found out that he was having online affairs. He was also addicted to online pornography. Again, I considered his stress to be a contributing factor to his unorthodox behavior

About two weeks before the wedding I began to have second thoughts about marrying him. My happiness dwindled. I began to feel the spirit of sadness. I experienced migraine headaches almost all the time because I was so stressed out. My fairytale was turning into a *horror movie*.

One day, I packed a bag on a mission to stay at my best friend's house because I felt like I just needed a break from it all. After she received me, we sat talking. I told her that I was canceling the wedding and that I did not want to go back to my house. After I poured out the full story from the 'fairytale flask' giving her a vivid picture of its taste, she too agreed that I should cancel the wedding. She also went on to recount noticing the negative way that my fiancé treated me; so of course she was in favor of my decision.

Then, few days later my fiancé and I talked. He apologized for his behavior, convincing me to come back home so that he could marry me; make me his wife. I believed that he was sorry. I accepted his apology and went back home.

A week or so before the wedding, my children came back from Buffalo so that they could prepare for the wedding. They seemed very sad. They did not want me to get married but did not know how to express their feelings because they were so young. But I could see it in their eyes. I knew deep down inside that I was making a huge mistake. Things never got better.

As we got closer to the wedding date my fiancés attitude towards me got worse. He would look at me with disgust and roll his eyes at me. He would say things like... *"You ain't all that."*

"I could do a lot better than you."

But, because I had been engaged several times in the past I was too embarrassed to cancel this wedding. I sent the invitations out, my family booked plane tickets and everyone was expecting a wedding. Not only that, but I was already become known as the runaway bride.

In past relationships, I would stand up to my boyfriends when they tried to be disrespectful or show any signs of abuse. I didn't take trash from anyone. But there was something about this man that scared me. I would never talk back to him. He would say things to hurt my feelings and I would just walk away and cry like a little girl. I thought that I deserved it and that I was doing something wrong.

The wedding day had finally arrived. Our family members all came in town just a few days earlier. To the world we appeared to be the perfect couple. We had been interviewed by the local newspaper and were featured on several websites for our wedding.

The wedding day had finally arrived. I did not get any sleep the night before. I was tired, cranky and wanted to run away. Just a few hours before the wedding I went to get my makeup done. I wanted to go alone. I needed time to myself and time to think. After getting my makeup done, I sat in my car for almost two hours having thoughts of not showing up at the wedding.

Before I knew it, it was time for the wedding to start. I took my time driving to the wedding location. Everyone was waiting for me so that the ceremony could start. Here, I wasn't even dressed yet. When I went to the room my dress hung was so overtaken by my emotions that I just stood there staring at it. Then, one of my cousins came into the room "What are you doing? Put your dress on, your husband to be is waiting for you."

I slowly put on the wedding dress and proceeded to the area where the ceremony was to take place. My dad was standing there waiting to give me away to a man who appeared to be 'the perfect' son-in-law. I must admit, I was a beautiful bride. Beautiful on the outside—but torn on the inside. Once the wedding processional began everyone stood up smiling.

As I walked down the spiral staircase to meet my soon to be husband, I had thoughts of running out of the side door. However, I maintained my composure, put on a fake smile and pretended to be happy. That walk down the aisle seemed like it was the longest walk I had ever taken. We looked each other in the eyes and said our vows like two people who were madly in love. We didn't even sleep together that night.

Though my past choices and chances were to make
others happy instead of considering myself...
I'm Still Standing

Choices and chances can be beneficial or costly.

Choices...

the act of choosing : the act of picking or deciding between two or more possibilities.

Chances...

an opportunity to do something : an amount of time or a situation in which something can be done.

*Merriam-webster.com
www.merriam-webster.com

Don't take the chance of continuing to suffer with abuse; make a choice to become a Survivor.

I choose to be a Survivor.
I'm Still Standing

{Wounds to Wisdom...I'm Still Standing}

TIME OUT:

Taking time out to reflect on the factors upon which you make your choices or take your chances can help you to make better decisions for your future.

www.tamikolowry.com

Chapter Eleven
THE HONEYMOON

The next day my new husband and I left for our honeymoon. We arrived in sunny Miami. It was my first time there, so I was excited about the beaches. I was also hoping that my husband and I could finally have some quality time together. I thought for sure that once on our honeymoon we would finally spark our connection and find a little bonding time. The first day was great. We browsed the streets of Miami, went to the beach, ate and shopped. Later that evening, I showered then put on my new lingerie for my husband. I felt *beautiful and sexy*.

However, when he saw me, he just rolled over and went to sleep. I cried most of the night. I had just been rejected by my husband. That would be the first of many times that my husband rejected me. I thought to myself, what's wrong with me? Am I ugly? Am I overweight? Am I doing something wrong?

After our honeymoon was over we went back home to start our new lives as *husband and wife*. A part of me was afraid to face the reality that I had made the biggest mistakes of my life.

During most of our first year of marriage my husband's sister along with her three children and my father-in-law all lived with us. Not to mention my husband had two children that visited on a regular basis so that made a total of eleven people in a four bedroom house.

Keep in mind, my husband and I were the only ones bringing in income, paying bills and buying food; which I believed was the major strain on our marriage. My husband would get very withdrawn at times; and even take his frustrations out on me.

Needless to say, I felt as though my life was a living hell. But, he was my husband now, so I had to keep quiet about it; view it as a package deal and do what I could to make him happy. Even if it meant for me to be unhappy.

Though my happy times didn't always make me feel "happy"...I'm Still Standing

Chapter Twelve

SLEEPING WITH THE ENEMY

"Sometimes we go backward only to delay or detour our forward blessings."

-Ingrid N. Allen

Over the course of the next three years my husband beat me emotionally, mentally, and verbally. He had been physical only a few times by choking or restraining me. There were incidents of infidelity by both of us. There are some things that I blocked out of my mind and I do not remember. And some things are too painful to relive at this moment. *These are the blank pages of my life...{Details Coming Soon}*

In November of 2006, I separated from my husband and moved into my own place. We sold our home and split the proceeds 50/50. My children and I were happy to be living in our own place away from all of the drama and heartache that we had encountered over the past few years. We felt free.

About a month or so after our separation, my husband begged me to go marriage counseling. I agreed to go and was hopeful that we could possibly make our marriage work. We went to one session in which we argued with each other the entire time. The minister who was counseling us looked like he was in shock. He told us that we had a long ways to go and separation may be a good choice for the time being. He also suggested that my husband try to get professional counseling because he felt that he had some deep rooted issues that needed to be addressed.

For the next month or so, my husband and I went on a few dates and decided that we would try to work things out. I really believed that things would be different and decided to give our marriage another shot before throwing in the towel. We went out and looked at houses until we found one that we both agreed on. During this time my husband seemed like a changed man. He was a gentleman. We would go on romantic dates and talk about what our future would be like. I really thought that he had made a change for the better.

In March of 2007, we moved into our new home. A seven bedroom four bathroom 3-story home. This was my dream home. *But*, the day that we moved in *'all hell'* broke loose. Once again, I questioned deep down inside if I was making a mistake.

The day that we moved into the new home, my mom and I unpacked boxes in the living room, while my children excitingly setup their rooms. My husband was also joined with us in the living room to hang the blinds on the windows.

As I looked over at him, I felt a warming feeling come over me. Just thinking of the positive possibilities I began to get really hopeful about getting back together with my husband. I was also very excited about building a new life in our new home. So, I grabbed a bottle of champagne and proposed a toast to *'new beginnings'*.

After pouring my mom a glass, she and I shared a toast, hug and a smile. My husband ignored me when I asked if he wanted to toast. I didn't think he heard me, so I walk closer to him handing him a glass of champagne. He turned to me and said *"Get that shit out of my face. Don't you see me hanging up the blinds?"*

At that moment, I turned to my mom with a puzzled look on my face—seeking comforting reassurance within her spirit. But before I could grasp ahold of her motherly inspiration, reality set in and I started crying.

As I sat back down next to my mother, she grabbed my hand gently whispering to me that everything would be *OK*.

"He was probably stressed out from the move."

"Give him time."

My feelings were hurt. All I wanted to do was to have a toast with my husband to celebrate our new home and our recommitment to one another. I sat on the floor for almost an hour crying. He never came to comfort me. He looked back at me, shook his head and kept on hanging up blinds. At this point, I knew he had not changed one bit.

Over the course of the next few weeks my husband's behavior revealed that he'd totally reverted back to his old ways. He became increasingly impatient and insulting. He never had anything nice to say to me. He was mean, condescending, and always acted as if he hated me.

When I expressed to him that I was unhappy and suggested that maybe we may have made a mistake by getting back together. He said *"No, we are gonna work this out!"*

Surprisingly, a few weeks later he decided that we should invite our friends and family over for a house warming party. [He always wanted to impress other people] So, I knew this was just to show off the new house. I really didn't care either way. I didn't even want to be there.

Nevertheless, we ended up having a huge housewarming party with over 100 guests. There was food, drinks, games for the children, and we even gave tours of the house. Our guest thought that we had it all together. They thought we were the perfect family. We had the house, the cars, and the look of a family who had it together. Yet deep down inside there was lots and lots of pain, resentment, and anger.

After the housewarming party was over things went back to the way they were. My husband and I hardly spoke to one another. He would force me to have sex with him when he wanted it. I was breaking down emotionally. Things got so bad that we didn't sleep in the same room anymore.

When he began to travel on a regular basis for work I loved my time alone. Having the house to myself gave me a sense of peace and freedom.

Seeing as though the kids were getting out of school for the summer I decided to send my son to stay with his dad in Atlanta and my daughter to Buffalo to be with my family.

While my children were gone, I made the choice to leave my husband for good. My plan was move into a place of my own before my children returned home. I wanted them to come home to a place free from violence, hate and anger.

When our anniversary came around we still were not on good terms. At that moment, I knew that it was time for me to go. However, the obstacle was finding safe, suitable living space for me and my children. I felt as if I were losing my sanity.

The Plan to Leave it All Behind

When my husband mentioned that he was leaving town for a business trip and would not return until the following Tuesday...I thought it would be a great time to plan my 'out'.

While he was gone I was going to wipe the house clean—taking all the furniture that I needed. I figured that I would put it into storage and move in with a friend until I found a place.

Senselessly, I procrastinated; and before I knew it Monday morning came. As I began to pack my mental baggage, the phone rang...it was my husband. He was calling to inform me that he was coming home early. Also, he wanted me to pick him up from the airport.

So, I thought that would be a perfect opportunity to let him know that I was leaving for good. When he got in the car he asked, "Why do you have a suitcase in the back seat?"

I told him that I was moving out and that I was not happy. His response was, "Maybe we should go have a drink and talk about it."

"I don't know what the problem is; but, I do not want to lose my wife."

Now keep in mind, this is the same man who would force himself on me for sex, tell me that I was not all that, call me names, and choke me on occasions. Why on earth would he want to save his marriage? I told him…No. I did not want to go have a drink. I just wanted to drop him off at home and go my separate way.

He told me that if I left him that he would kill both of us. He then tried to take the steering wheel and make us crash. We were on GA Interstate 85 near the Atlanta airport, driving at least 70 mph. Yet, somehow managed to pull the car over to the side of the road.

Once the car was in the park position, he proceeded to choke, punch and slap me. Still, not sure how I ended in the passenger seat all I remember is trying to open the door. But, he kept pounding my hand with his fist to move it from the door handle. The pain was excruciating. As a result of this my ring finger on my right hand was broken.

After that I must have went unconscious because the only that I could recall was getting up off the ground in the middle of the highway. There were cars swerving and blowing their horns so that they would not hit me.

All I was wearing was my bra and a pair of black slacks. I have no idea how my blouse came off. There was a couple in a car parked behind ours who informed me that they called the police. In the meantime, my husband was yelling at me telling me to get my ass in the car so that he could take me home. I refused to get in the car. I thought he was going to kill me.

Just a few minutes later, the police showed up. He ran over to one of the officers screaming that I attacked him for no reason. I was crying hysterically trying to tell the police that he was lying and that he had actually attacked me.

My husband had scratches on his face and neck only due to me trying to protect myself from him. My bruises were not yet visible, so it was apparent that the police were taking his side asking me why he had bruises and I didn't. I began to sob harder pleading with the police officers to listen to me as I attempted to choke out what happened. They told me that if I didn't calm down that they were going to take me to jail. *A classic example of blaming the victim.*

Thankfully, the people who had called the police gave their version of what they saw. So, the police handcuffed my husband and placed him in the back of the police car. The police officer then asked me to fill out a form describing the incident that had taken place. While filling out the report there on the hood of the police car, I noticed my husband in the back seat laughing hysterically like a mad man. Then, he started using his body to shake the car, yelling saying *"I'm not finished with you yet bitch!"*

Once the police took him off to jail, I got in the car and went back to our home. I was going to try to pack up as much stuff as possible but I was afraid and paranoid that my husband would walk in the door any minute. Even though I knew he had gone to jail I still did not feel safe.

I left the house and went to my mom's place. I laid on her couch the entire night crying trying to figure out *why* this had to happen to me.

During this time my husband and I worked for the same company. So after the last incident took place I informed an administrator at job that I had a restraining order against my husband.

Therefore, we were not permitted to work within the same building or be in specific proximity of each other. Though the administrator was receptive to my request [based on company protocol] the company was required to perform an investigation.

A few days later, I was called down to a meeting with a representative from the Human Resources Department. They advised me to immediately change my phone number and my phone plan because my husband had been tracking and monitoring my calls for the past four years.

He had also placed a GPS device in my car; which was used to track my whereabouts. It literally blew my mind that he was using company equipment to stalk me all these years.

Seeing as though he violated company policy by using their equipment to stalk me he was immediately terminated.

Within a month of the incident I found a place to live; which was directly down the street from my job. When my children came home from summer vacation we had a new place to live. I was not sure how I was going to pay my bills and make it as a single parent because I was used to having a combined income with my husband. But, I didn't care. All I wanted was *peace of mind*.

Although I had a restraining order, my husband continued to try to contact me. He would call me constantly and write me letters. He was still living in our home and refused to give me any furniture including my children's clothing and bed sets. I had to get a court order and go to the house with a police escort in order to retrieve some of the items.

Approximately two months after the incident, I was finally able to go to the house with the police escort. When my husband opened the door he didn't look quite 'himself'. He had obviously lost a lot of weight, looked stressed and sick.

As we walked in the house I could hear the sounds of Musiq Soulchild (*Teach Me How to Love*) playing on repeat throughout the house. It was a very eerie and creepy feeling. I walked into the kitchen there were pictures of us that we had taken over the years including wedding pictures. They were lined up across the kitchen counter.

I went upstairs to our bedroom to retrieve some clothing there was a vase of flowers on the dresser for me with a note that read… *"I miss you and I'm sorry."*

There also was another note next to the flowers that read… *"Turn on the TV."* So, I turned on the television, only to see our wedding video playing. This had to be the wackiest thing I had experienced. My husband was obviously experiencing some serious mental issues.

Then, at one point while the police officer was downstairs my husband came upstairs while I was getting my clothes out of the closet. It frightened me when he came in the closet with me, closing the door behind him. I thought for sure he was going to try to hurt me. But he grabbed me and tried to hug me tight. I screamed for "help" and the police came upstairs instructing him to go back downstairs.

A few days after, I was served divorce papers on my job. Shocked... but thankful that he went ahead with the process. Then, next day he called saying that he did it as a scare tactic to get me back. Well, it didn't work. All I wanted was a divorce. No alimony or anything else. Just a divorce, my freedom. My peace of mind. *My life.*

The Challenges & Blessings of Survivorship

Starting over was difficult. I was not making enough money to make ends meet. There were days when I would steal my coworkers' lunches from the break room to take home and feed my children.

Things got so bad that one time, after an employee cookout I stole a huge, (unopened) 100 count box of hotdogs that were left over. My children and I ate off of those for almost a month.

I can also recall a time when I did not have any money for food or gas. My gas tank was almost on empty. It was a Sunday morning and I really wanted to go to church; so I decided to take the chance and drive to church on an empty tank.

As I sat in the pews listening to 'the word', I began to cry out to God asking for "help".

Then, out of nowhere a man sitting next to me [whom I had never seen before] handed me $20. He said *"God told me to bless you with this."*

Keep in mind, I never saw that man ever again. He must have been an angel in disguise.

That same day after service was over, I went to the finance committee and asked if I could have my $100 back from a deposit that I made for an upcoming women's retreat. Since I could not afford to pay the remaining balance it just made sense to get my deposit back so that I could buy groceries for my family. But, they told me that my deposit was non-refundable. I explained to them that I had just left an abusive marriage and that I had no money for food. They still refused to give me a refund.

It wasn't until I burst out into a hysterical crying outrage in the foyer of the church that they decided to give me back my deposit. At that point I was outraged at the church.

In April of 2008, we finally had our divorce hearing. My husband looked at me and told me that I looked amazing. And told me that he would give me another chance if I wanted it. I looked at him and smiled and said "Although that statement should be the other way around, I decline your offer."

I signed my divorce papers and walked out a free woman. I had my life back. For the first time, I had stood up to my husband without crying or getting over emotional. My husband was not my ex-husband. He was now a part of my past.

Financially things were tough. From the time I left my ex-husband until early 2009, I had been evicted (not once, not twice) three times. I was barely making ends meet and could not afford my bills let alone my rent.

In my divorce decree my ex-husband was ordered to pay my car payment for the truck that he purchased for me during our marriage. Of course he didn't pay. So, on my way to work one day I went outside only to find my car repossessed.

It hurt to know that he would not keep up the payments, however I looked at it as God removing him totally from my life. This way I was no longer dependent nor obligated to him. I was on a mission to build a life for myself and my children on my own.

"Overcoming financial hardship helped me to be a better financial steward."
I'm, Still Standing

Chapter Thirteen
WISDOM

For the next few months, I cried out to God to give me an answer as to *why* I had to go through these painful hard times. Why me God?! Why me? Why did I have to go through and emotionally and physically abusive childhood? Why did I have to go through an abusive relationship as a teenager? Why did I have sexually assaulted? Why did my best friend get killed by her abusive boyfriend? Why was I a statistic as a teenage mother? Why was I a victim of Domestic Violence? Why God? *Why me?*

On August 9th 2009, I sat in the pew at Grace Church International Church asking God why me? My pastor was preaching a sermon on turning your pain into purpose.

"God didn't deliver you from that abusive relationship for nothing." He said.

"There was a reason behind it." "There is purpose out of that pain."

It was one of those moments when you think they are talking directly to you. He was preaching from Romans 8:28 *"And we know for those who love God all things work together for good, for those who are called according to his purpose."* At that moment I knew my purpose in life.

Tears began to flow as I thanked and praised God for turning my pain into purpose. My wounds now became my wisdom. The wisdom that I would share with thousands of women around the world who were going through what I went through. You see God has a plan for each and every one of us. No matter what you situation may be, no matter what it is that you are going through it will eventually work together and become your purpose.

Now, I know my purpose in life. What do I do next? How do I accomplish what God said I'm supposed to do? How will I reach these women that God said I'm supposed to help? One day God spoke to me, he said start a nonprofit organization. Through this organization you are going to help thousands of women. They will look to you for guidance and direction. I thought to myself, really God. How am I supposed to do this?

What will I call it? Who is going to help me? I don't know anything about starting a nonprofit organization. I felt God speaking to me saying "Just do it!" Over the course of the next 3 months I would jot down different names that I thought should be the name of my organization—none of them seemed to be right. So, I *stopped* and *prayed.* I asked God what the name should be. He didn't answer immediately. In November of 2009, I went on a date with a gentleman that I was not sure that I even liked. During our date I shared some of my trials and tribulations with him and he shared his with me.

During our conversation he stood up and said, "You know what?" "After all that we have been through, we are still standing!" At that moment I jumped up and hugged him. I said *"That's it, that's it."* "The name of my organization is going to be The Still Standing Foundation." Needless to say, our relationship didn't work out; but I did get the name of my organization from it. I'm not sure if that was orchestrated by God or not, however it worked out for my good.

The realization and manifestation
of my destiny came when I least expected.
I'm Still Standing

Survival Talk-

TOPIC of DISCUSSION

Wisdom

- *Wisdom is....?*
- *Explain how your life's experiences have shaped your views of wisdom?*
- *Understanding that the wounds of your reality were meat for a purpose. –Wisdom*

Chapter Fourteen

STILL STANDING

Psalm 62:2
Truly he is my rock and my salvation;
he is my fortress, I will not be shaken.

Standing and believing in Survivorship

—Wounds to Wisdom...I'm Still Standing

A Purposeful Mission and a Will of Survival

At this point, I knew my purpose. I had a name for my organization. But, I still didn't quite know where these women were going to come from that I was destined to help. So with Facebook and Twitter as a resource—I began to promote the Still Standing Foundation.

Every day I would submit a morning meditation or something inspirational to empower the people that visited my page. I also posted domestic violence information and statistics that I felt would be beneficial to those who were going through domestic violence. Likewise, noting inspirational wellness tips for those who were working their Will of Survival plan. Some were so inspired by my postings that they began to call me the *'Empowering Diva'* [which is now branded as my Twitter handle].

Needless to say, as a result of the social media promotion both The Still Standing Foundation and I currently have thousands of Followers on both our Twitter and Facebook pages. We are *all things survivor*—survival of the mind, body and spirit.

Today, [five years] later, The Still Standing Foundation has become a nationally known organization. We serve hundreds of women and teenagers each year via workshops, seminars and speaking engagements throughout the country.

- In 2012, we were awarded the Atlanta Rising in Community Excellence Award
- Subsequently in 2013, we were honored at the Atlanta "Best of" Non Profit award.
- Then in 2014, we were awarded the Atlanta History Maker Award.

In addition, on May of 2013, we were blessed to cut the ribbon to our first office and are now looking forward to continuing our mission globally as advocates for Domestic Violence Awareness for years to come.

As I come to a close with this book … I think about how things could have been different within my life. Yet, I wouldn't change a thing (*ok*, maybe one or two things). But, the moral of the story is, I survived.

Not, just for me, but rather for the purpose of my calling and the fulfillment of my destiny. To stand as a survivor with others so that we become a strong unit to help heal this nation of domestic abuse. To educate, encourage and empower women and men all over the world as they walk boldly into survivorship in all areas of their lives.

With praises to God, whom I give thanks for the
blessing to have survived by his grace and mercy.
I'm Still Standing

TIME OUT:

Taking time out to get to know the 'inner' you is important to your overall wellness. If you don't know who you are how can anyone else get to know you?

Though your past experiences may have not been 'the best" it does not mean that you can't redesign your future.

Draw the 'blueprint' of your future.
Then, take action as you seek to
discover the *'new'* you.

www.tamikolowry.com

"My wounds have made me wiser."

**I've learned to be wiser in my choices,
so that I am more at peace.**

I'm Still Standing

Survivorship is Wellness…

I'M STILL STANDING

Essential Wellness Principles
to Help You Live a Winning Lifestyle

- Pray
- Praise
- Meditate
- Eat Healthy
- Exercise
- Get Rest
- Set Goals—Short Term & Long Term
- Learn/Train/Study
- Construct a Financial Plan to Help You Budget and Become a Good Steward Over Your Financial Blessings
- Spend Quality Time with Friends & Family
- Feed Your Spirit Good Energy
- Take Time Out for Yourself
- Explore New Opportunities
- Be Mindful of Doing Things that You **Like to Do** vs. Just Those that You **Have to Do**
- Explore Your Gifts & Talents
- Smile/Laugh Often (*it soothes the soul*)
- Speak Good Things into Existence in Your Life
- Stay Positive/Surround Yourself with Positivity

Realize that abuse is NEVER your fault.

Hurt people, hurt people; this is why healing from abuse is so important to your wellness. It helps to prevent the cycle of hurt, abuse and disparity.

(Proclaim that your life will never be the same)

Survivorship is Real…

I'M STILL STANDING

"The love and sacrifice of family is truly priceless." —
We're Still Standing

Tamiko with Son (Michael)

Tamiko with Daughter (Destiny)

Tamiko with Mom

Tamiko with Dad

Tamiko with Sisters-Danielle and Aishah Lowry

"Stand for a cause; witness an effect."—

We're Still Standing!

Tamiko with Amber Lyons-Founder of From Pain to Purpose

Tamiko with Domestic Violence Advocates

Tamiko with Ashley Nicole

"Surrounding yourself with positive people helps to inspire, encourange and support the mission."—
We're Still Standing!

SSF Back To School Supply Drive

"The Power of Prayer, Patience, and Unconditionally Loving Mentorship."— We're Still Standing!

Tamiko with Co-Pastor & Mentor Dr. Toni Alvarado

"Talent, Wisdom and Experience surrounds us to help us grow and develop into lifetime Survivors." —
We're Still Standing!

Tamiko with Minister Kenny Pugh-Author, Finance Coach

Tamiko with Deborah Hightower-Speaker, Entertainer

Tamiko with Mimi Johnson-MimiJohnson.net

Tamiko with Jack A. Daniels-Author Speaker, Coach

*"Awareness and community involvement helps to
promote Survivorship"* —
We're Still Standing!

Tamiko with Erin Coleman- WSB Atlanta TV News

Solicitor General Sherry Boston Senator Jason Carter

Stop Violence Against Women Day 2014

"Surviving is believing!"—
We're Still Standing!

Black Dress Affair Honoring Cancer Survivors

The Still Standing Foundation
Empowering Victims to Become Survivors

Rising Star Awards

Still Standing Supporters

The Still Standing Foundation
Atlanta Office Ribbon Cutting Celebration
2013

"Support, encoragement and inspiration gives us hope to survive."—
We're Still Standing!

SSF Buffalo, NY Supporters

SSF Supporters

A Special 'Thanks' to all of the Supporters of
The Still Standing Foundation.

We are Still Standing...

Empowering victims to become survivors!

Still Standing Workout Crew-Atlanta, GA

SSF Teen Dating Workshop-Atlanta, GA

SSF Survivors

Freedom Workshop

*"God's purpose will forever live on
through Survivorship."*—
We're Still Standing!

Red Pump Event for HIV Awareness

"Wisdom is not always measured by what you know but rather how you embrace your wounds of experiences."

-Tamiko Lowry

I have forgiven so that I too can be forgiven.
I'm Still Standing

Author Contact:
www.tamikolowry.com

Wounds-to-Wisdom helps to educate and empower; so that victims can identify, embrace and enjoy survivorship of Domestic Abuse.

–Ingrid N. Allen

A Women Standing in Purpose through Wounds of Wisdom...

"I'm Still Standing as a testament of God's love and the hope of a calling. Therefore, as a soldier of great missions my life has been purposed to empower victims to become survivors."
—Tamiko Lowry

ABOUT THE AUTHOR

Tamiko Lowry, is a survivor...

After years of hurdling over obstacles and roadblocks including a marriage in which her spirit, mind, and body was battered constantly, she has embarked on a journey to birth purpose out of her pain. A Buffalo, NY native, Tamiko Lowry is the epitome of her aptly named non-profit, The Still Standing Foundation—an organization that provides a positive outlet for survivors of domestic violence to shed the shame and despair of their struggle while gaining strength and power in spite of it. She is a compassionate mentor and friend, an enthusiastic leader, and visionary.

As a Speaker, Empowerment Life Coach, and Domestic Violence Advocate, Tamiko believes that empowerment comes from within and can be achieved by honoring yourself, your values, and expressing your talents and gifts.

As an Author, Lowry is committed to principals of wellness (mind, body and spirit). Therefore, with healing in mind, she shares her personal journey, **Wounds—to—Wisdom...*I'm Still Standing*** as a testament of survival; to touch the emotional barriers of its reading audience and give hope to those that have [or are experiencing] Domestic Abuse.

Tamiko is a member of The National Association of Professional Women, Atlanta's Urban Professionals, Atlanta Women Entrepreneurs (AWE), and Women in The Spotlight GoinGlobal.

In 2010, she was featured in Career Magazine's article *"40 Movers and Shakers under the age of 40"*. Also, in 2012 Tamiko received The Celebration of Gospel Atlanta Rising Star Award for her work with the Still Standing Foundation. She recently received the Atlanta Black History Makers Award.

Tamiko also serves as a contributor for the Gospel Tribune Atlanta, and the Fulton County Women's Journal. Wisdom gained from experience has also afforded her many opportunities to appear on several radio and talk shows, host seminars, workshops, and provide support to other charitable organizations throughout the country.

Tamiko currently resides in Atlanta, GA where she celebrates and enjoys her survivorship with her two children Michael & Destiny.

Wounds to Wisdom...I'm Still Standing by Tamiko Lowry
www.tamikolowry.com

Tamiko is a strong voice of empowerment for those that are experiencing Domestic Abuse.

Founder of The Still Standing Foundation & Certified Life Coach
Tamiko Lowry

Wounds to Wisdom
I'm Still Standing
An inspiring tool of empowerment for surviving Domestic Abuse.

MORE TITLES COMING SOON!

www.tamikolowry.com
Email the Author:
woundstowisdomthebook@gmail.com

To order bulk quantities or wholesale for retail send email requests
to **sales@thewritersmagic.com**
The Writers' Magic Books (USA)
Atlanta, Georgia
www.thewritersmagic.com

Wounds to Wisdom
shares an intimate view of a purposeful journey won by the power of love, healing and faith...

"Educational, Inspirational and Empowering."

Wounds to Wisdom...
I'm Still Standing
By
TAMIKO LOWRY

"Though Domestic Abuse may hurt or bruise, it does not have to leave us broken."

*Wounds-to-Wisdom...*I'm Still Standing
A journey & testament of hope, purpose and destiny.

Throughout the course of our lives we are often faced with many situations and circumstances that may cause us to become wounded—physically, emotionally, mentally, financially and even spiritually. However, those bumps & bruises do not have to leave us broken.

Dedicated to survivors all over the world and to those whom have lost their lives, we respectfully tribute...Mothers, Sisters, Brothers, Fathers, Children & Friends.

The Writers' Magic.

Writing & Publishing Consultancy

A Global Resource Network for Writers & Creators

THE WRITERS' MAGIC BOOKS

Print/eBooks/Audio Books

www.thewritersmagic.com
*Find out about manuscript submission

Unleash the Magic within with The Writer's Magic!

Bulk quantities are available at a discounted rate for book clubs or special events. For more information please contact us at
sales@thewritersmagic.com

The Writers' Magic Books (USA)
Atlanta, Georgia
www.thewritersmagic.com

Abuse is Never Ok...

If you or someone that you love are experiencing abuse get help with a survival plan before it's too late.

The National Domestic Violence Hotline
1-800-799-7233
1-800-787-3224 TTY

www.thehotline.org

The Still Standing Foundation
www.thestillstandingfoundation.org

Made in the USA
Charleston, SC
22 January 2015